BONZO'S

COMPLETE BOOK of SKITS

(Volume 1)

by Barry DeChant

BONZO PRODUCTIONS
LIVONIA, MICHIGAN

Cover design by b. j. Graphics, Ypsilanti, MI

Copyright ©1997 Barry K. DeChant
All rights reserved. No part of this book may be reproduced in any form, except for brief reviews, without written permission of the publisher.

Bonzo Productions
14209 Ingram
Livonia, Michigan 48154
USA

Library of Congress Cataloging-in-Publication Data
DeChant, Barry K., 1937
   Bonzo's Complete Book of Skits (vol. I) by Barry DeChant

   ISBN 0-9659211-0-7
     1. Clowns   2. Amateur Plays. I. Title

Library of Congress Catalog Card Number
97-73580

Published and printed in the United States of America

PREFACE

This book is divided by number of clowns needed for the skits. There are gags for use by a single clown and some skits where an <u>unlimited</u> number of clowns may be involved. The only limits you will have are the ones you place on yourself.

I encourage you to read the skits/gags, discuss them with friends, make modifications to customize them for your specific needs, rehearse them a lot, and have fun entertaining all of your audiences.

We can all learn from others, even those who have been our former students. With that in mind, I dedicate this book to my friend and former partner, Ron 'SNUDEK' Kardynski. He was one of my students, many years ago, and has expanded his clowning skills beyond all parameters. He has encouraged and taught me new endeavors in clowning and has been a personal inspiration. I thank him for his dedication to our wonderful Art of Clowning.

TABLE OF CONTENTS

SKITS and GAGS

What are skits? 1
Why perform skits? 2
The Elements of a Skit 4
Preparing to Perform 7
In Conclusion 9

SKITS for ONE CLOWN

Disappearing Cracker 11
Don't Bug Me 13
Magic Scarves 18
Standing On A Cup 19
Walk Arounds 22

SKITS for TWO CLOWNS

Cotton Candy 25
Disappearing Water 27
Dog and Hoop 30
Hamburger Stand 32
Have a Seat 40
High Diver 41
Just One Hand 44
On A Date 46
Paint Company 49
Painters 51
Pizza Man 54
Right Toe 56
Sharpshooter 57
Stagecoach 59
Telephone Call 61

TABLE OF CONTENTS (cont'd)

SKITS for TWO CLOWNS

Tumblers 65
Two on a Chair 67
Washday 70
What Time is it? 73
Whipcracker 74

SKITS FOR THREE CLOWNS

Space Age Cleaner 79
The Box 82
Levitation 86
Mary Had a Little Lamb 88
Long Shirt 91
Strongman 95
Fire, Fire 97

SKITS FOR FOUR or MORE CLOWNS

Mary Had a Little Lamb 100
Cheerleader 105
Construction Company 106
Teeterboard 108
Seascape (a story) 111
Restaurant 114
Twelve Days of Clowning 117

SKITS or GAGS
The Art of Clown Performing

WHAT ARE SKITS?

A long time ago…there was an Auguste clown who had never gotten a laugh for himself. He had been clowning for about 15 years, and was depressed with the situation. It seemed like every other clown in the alley was getting laughs, but him.

One night, he was a little slow getting out of the ring…when the elephants entered. An elephant actually stepped on his foot…and just stood there. The clown tried pushing the elephant off…he pleaded with the elephant to move…and finally he screamed…hit…and bit the elephant. He did everything he could think of to get the elephant off of his foot.

After a couple of agonizing minutes, the trainer got the elephant off…and the clown was carried from the arena by two other clowns. All the while the audience was roaring with laughter, and gave the clown a standing ovation as he was carried out. There were even a few shouts of 'encore.'

As you can see **IRONY** is an important part of clown skits (or 'gags' as they are called in the circus). Ironies like falling off of a ladder…spilling paint on yourself or another clown…having a cake explode in your face…getting hit with pies or water…or even slipping on a banana peel. When these thing happen to 'normal' people they are not necessarily seen as funny, but when they happen to a clown there are seen as outrageous.

That's what most skits are all about. Everyday events that don't go the way we expect to see them. Exaggeration of events...misinterpretations...parodies of other entertainment...and parodies of skills. They all appear as entertaining to our audiences IF they are well rehearsed and presented in a professional manner.

Most skits are like stories. They have a plot...and progress to a (hopefully) funny ending.

WHY PERFORM SKITS?

ENTERTAINMENT is the primary reason, although skits may also be used to:

1. Convey a message to your audience
   - Political Message
   - Religious Message (Clown Ministry)
   - Teaching Message (Safety, Say NO to drugs)

2. Skits can be seen by large audiences who need to be entertained. They can fill a large stage or circus ring.

3. They allow us to have 'fun' performing our skills.

4. They can include slapstick and messiness that cannot be done in small confined areas.

Although skits require relatively large areas for performing, they are a very special element of our craft. They cannot replace the close-up magic, balloon sculpture, face-painting, and other one-on-one clown opportunities, but they are another facet of clowning that all clowns should be familiar with. They usually require interacting with other clowns, and thus require rehearsal and preparation time.

For the most part, skits usually require two or more clowns, but they can utilize an unlimited number of clowns depending on the writing and performance techniques applied.

You can get ideas for skits by watching people in such places as shopping malls, fairs, churches, on public transportation, and most anywhere that people gather. Watch the way people react to situations. What do they do? Why do you think they react in a particular way? Put your clown character in the same situation and predict how your clown would react to the same situation. Would he/she keep trying the same thing, or would your clown do it in a different way? Try to see the humorous possibilities in the event.

Specific occupations lend themselves to skit opportunities. Try to think of various occupations and see how your clown would react. A fireman working at a fire, a police officer directing traffic, a dentist office, a street cleaner (do these occupations still exist?), a restaurant waiter, etc. There a limitless possibilities for your imagination.

THE ELEMENTS OF A SKIT:

There are three specific elements that every successful skit **must** contain, just like telling a good story. They are:

1. Beginning - This sets the scene for the situation. It introduces the characters to the audience. It lets them know the location for the action.

2. Middle - This is the actual telling of the story. It puts the action in motion. This is where the plot builds toward the conclusion. It sets the story line and usually involves some sore of conflict:
   Clown vs. Clown
   Clown vs. Object
   Clown vs. Situation

3. Ending - This is usually referred to as the Blow-Off or the 'conclusion' of the story. In a joke this would be the punch-line. Without a good ending the skit falls apart...and the audience is left wondering if the skit is really over. This is a very important part of every skit.

There are several types of endings which include:
Logical Conclusion -
    What the audience expects.
Surprise Conclusion -
    What the audience does not expect.

Blow-Offs can be:
    A pie in the face
    A Chase-Off
    Someone hit with water
    Slaps, Kicks in the Pants
    Pants drops and chase off
    Explosions, pyrotechnics

In addition to the structure of the skit, additional appeals to the senses of the audience are important.

These include Music, Sound-Effects, Props, Costumes, Lighting, etc.

MUSIC: This is a very important element to include. It can set the **mood** of the skit...fast, happy, solemn, calm, etc.

PROPS: Make and use as many as you need to enhance your message. Make them colorful, sturdy, and safe. You don't want the prop falling apart in the middle of your gag, and you don't want yourself or your fellow clowns being injured by unsafe props.

If you have to transport the props, construct them so they can be disassembled for shipping and/or transporting.

They should accentuate the action, not detract from it.

Don't build and entire restaurant, if a chef's hat will do. Be careful not to **overprop** a skit.

If one rubber chicken is funny...two rubber chickens are not necessarily twice as funny.

Sound-Effects-

These go along with music to enhance your skit, but you must be careful to use them at **exactly** the correct moment.
They aren't funny if used too early or too late.

Lighting- This is one of the more difficult items for you to control. If the stage has lights, use them as best you can. If you can transport your own lighting system, be sure the performance area can handle the amount of electricity you require.
You don't want to blow a fuse in the middle of your act. **FOLO-SPOTS** can greatly enhance your performance, if they are available.

Costumes - Use these to create the location and situation you need. A chef's apron, cowboy hat, a fireman's hat. These costumes will tell your audience what and who you are trying to portray.

Talking - You've must be heard to be understood. If you are performing a skit that has dialogue, be sure you are speaking loud enough so that the <u>farthest</u> member of the audience can **hear** and **understand** you correctly.

PREPARING TO PERFORM:

It is important in **any** skit work that you consider the following:
1. Where will the skit be performed?
2. What facilities will be available? (stage, living room, etc.)
3. What props will you need?
4. How many clowns will be involved?
5. Is music appropriate, and playback equipment available?

As you begin preparation, use the same criteria that journalists use when preparing a story.
Who, What, When, Where, Why, and How

WHO - is in the skit...is in the audience?
WHAT - will you use? An existing skit or will you write a new one?
WHEN - will you perform (morning, afternoon, evening). In 1 month, 6 months, 1 yr.?

WHERE - will it be performed...stage...set of risers...shopping mall...auditorium?
WHY - are you doing it? For income, for experience, for competition?
HOW - will you do it? This book will give you many ideas to answer this item.

REHEARSE with your audience location in mind. Tell everyone in the skit that "The audience is over there" so you will know which direction to face and perform to.

Be sure your audience is **with** you. That they are looking where you want them to look. That they see the action you want them to see.

There are several ways to get the audience **with** you. Most things in our everyday life are based on **horizontal** events. Anything **vertical** will attract the audience's attention (such as a helium balloon being released or a body dropping). Loud noises will attract the audience attention...like an explosion...car horn...whistle...etc.

THE MAGIC THREES:

Psychologists and comedy writers have discovered the magic of the number three. If something is done three times, the comedy effect works. If it is done twice or more than three times, it doesn't work as well.

The formula is this: **Build up, Build up, Blow-Off**
To test this theory, watch your favorite sit-com on television. You will notice that most comedy effects use this "**magic of three**" formula.

What is actually happening is what psychologists call **Set Induction**. This means that when something happens the same way for a series of times, we begin to expect it to happen that way <u>every</u> time. By doing something, and having the same result twice in a row...the audience 'expects' it to happen the same way the third time. That element of the surprise change on the third time is what makes if funny...and unexpected.

The More the Merrier...is not necessarily true!!

Just because you have a lot of clowns in your group, is not a valid reason to <u>use</u> them all. When too many clowns are involved in the skit...they tend to get in the way and cause confusion for the audience. As a result, the audience does not know where to look and the extra clowns can actually block the skit from the audience line of sight. This makes it impossible for them to see what you are doing. This is definitely <u>not</u> funny for your audience.

IN CONCLUSION

The skits in this book cover a wide array of props, number of clowns needed, and clowning experience required.

They can be used exactly as explained, or can be modified and 'personalized' for your performance. I urge you to read them, try them, and have fun performing them.

May there always be a CLOWN in your life!!

Skits for One Clown

Disappearing Cracker

Number of Clowns:	One
Characters:	Clown Magician
Costumes:	Normal Wardrobe or maybe a magician's cape
Props:	Saltine or Animal Cracker
Stage:	Empty

ACTION: Clown enters dramatically and announces that he has perfected a new magic act. "Would you like to see it?" No matter what the response, he continues. "This trick involves nothing more that an ordinary saltine (or animal) cracker. Yet, I will make this cracker disappear right before your eyes". At this point someone may yell out that he's going to eat the cracker, but the clown announces, "That wouldn't be magic. I'm not going to eat the cracker...but I <u>will</u> make it disappear". He may wish to select a volunteer from the audience to inspect the cracker to make sure it doesn't have any trick mechanisms to it, and to re-assure the rest of the audience that it is, indeed, an ordinary cracker.

The clown then holds the cracker between his thumb and middle finger of one hand, palm upwards. He passes his other hand over the one holding the cracker, <u>pretending</u> to grab the cracker in the second hand.

Actually he drops the cracker into the open palm of his first hand, closes the palm, thus crumbling the cracker into his hand. He holds his second hand in the air, pointing to it with the first hand, and announces that he will now make it disappear, but he must first sprinkle it with the magic 'whiffle' dust.

He takes his other hand...pretends to grab some 'whiffle' dust from the air...holds his hand over the second hand...and sprinkles the 'whiffle' dust (crushed cracker) over the hand. He then opens the second hand to show the audience that, indeed, the cracker has disappeared. He takes a quick bow...and makes a fast exit.

DON'T BUG ME

Number of Clowns: One

Characters: Tramp, or Normal Clown

Costumes: Trampish

Props: 2 Fly Swatters, Spray Fumigator, Broom, Small Blanket, Bag for carrying props, "Rigged" hat.

Stage: Empty

ACTION: Clown (dressed as camper or man-of-the-road) enters when music begins.

He is carrying knapsack (or other type of bag) slung over his shoulder. This bag contains his 'belongings'. He is also carrying a broom. He looks around for a resting spot on the ground, and finally decides on a spot...sweeps it with his broom...takes out a blanket and lays down for a nap. He covers himself with the blanket. After a moment he hears the sound of an annoying mosquito buzzing around (tape sounds) and he shoos it away with his hand. (sound ends). He covers himself with blanket again and tries to go back to sleep.

After a moment, the mosquito returns. This time the clown swings his hand at the invisible mosquito, trying to get it. He lies back down as the mosquito sound fades away.

In a few seconds the mosquito reappears. The clown starts to get up, but he lies back down as the sound stops. In a moment he jumps, realizing that the mosquito has stopped, 'landed' <u>on him</u>, and has just bit him. He jumps around, scratches...and tries to get the mosquito with two fly-swatters from his bag. Mosquito sound ends...and clown lies back down covering himself with blanket again.

Soon he hears the pesky friend again. This time he gets up and gets a fumigator from the knapsack. He 'chases' the mosquito around trying to spray it. While doing so, the buzzing changes to music (Flight of the Bumblebee), and clown continues to chase the bug. Finally he 'sees' it land, and attempts to smash it with the fumigator just as the music ends. He again tries to go back to sleep.

In moments the mosquito returns. This time the clown gets up, looks to the sky and is trying to locate the mosquito. Soon the mosquito sound changes to the sound of a dive bomber plane. The clown picks up his broom, takes a stance like a baseball player at bat, and is ready to swing the broom at the incoming mosquito (bomber). He takes a couple of 'warm up' swings to let the audience know what he intends to do to the mosquito. The 'dive bomber mosquito' is coming closer and he is nervous, but determined to 'hit' him out of the park. His eyes follow the mosquito toward the bat. Just as he is about to swing, the dive bombers come to a 'screeching stop' (car screech) and his eyes follow the mosquito to the ground, at his feet.

He now feels his problems are over, and he returns to his blanket to catch some sleep.

In moments the mosquito returns. The clown gets up and follows it's flight with his eyes. When he sees it 'land' on the ground, he sneaks up to it, and places his (rigged) hat over it. In about 3 seconds the hat **EXPLODES** (smoke and flash powder) and the clown, standing nearby, is happy. He approaches the hat and lifts the back corner, expecting to see the dead mosquito. Instead he is surprised to hear the mosquito sounds again as the 'angry mosquito' flies out of the hat. The clown grabs his mat...and other belongings and is chased off the stage by the imaginary angry mosquito.

HAT CONSTRUCTION:

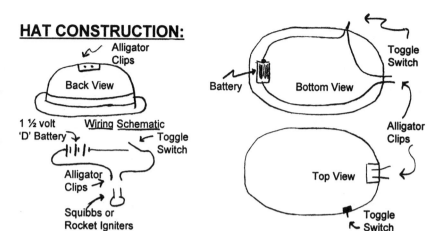

NOTE: Make metal 'box' from cutting metal and bending it into box shape. Attach to hat with bolts, otherwise it will blow out of the hat when explosion goes off. Use 1½ volt battery. This low voltage battery gives you a little bit of time to get across the stage before explosion occurs. Use explosive powder of your choice. CAUTION; This skit, as with any skit using pyrotechnics, must be done with extreme care, and persons not experienced with explosives should not attempt this skit.

EXTRA NOTE; If you don't have the 'rigged' hat or are uncomfortable working with pyrotechnics, you could take your broom and smash the hat when you feel you have the mosquito trapped under it.

MUSIC TRACK SEQUENCE:

:35	Music	Clown enters, finds spot, and lies down
:11	Buzzing	Clown looks up and shoos mosquito away
:09	Silence	Lies back down

Time	Sound	Action
:13	Buzzing	Swings hand at bug
:06	Silence	Lies back down
:06	Buzzing	Starts to get up, lies back down as buzzing stops. Waits then jumps up when he realizes he has been stung.
:05	Silence	Lies back down
:12	Buzzing	Jumps around, scratches, tries to get bug with fly swatters.
:09	Silence	Lies back down
:31	Buzzing and fade to music	Gets up, chases bug with fumigator and tries to hit it as music ends
:08	Silence	Lies back down
:19	Buzzing chng. to airplane	Gets up, looks skyward, hears plane, gets broom attempts to hit incoming bug.
:02	Screech	Starts to swing but stops, waits, and sees bug fall at his feet.
:05	Silence	Lies back down
:09	Buzzing	Sees bug fly around and watches it

:23	Silence	Sneaks up on bug and puts his hat over it.
		Flips switch for explosives (if used) or...smashes hat with broom.
:15	Funeral March	Sneaks up on hat and lifts a corner
:16	Buzzing	Mosquito chases clown off stage.

** Pre-recorded Cassette Tape for this skit is available from the author.

Magic Scarves

Number of Clowns: One

Characters: Magician

Costumes: Normal Clown

Props: Top hat, Table, 6 bandannas (3 colors...2 of each color)

Stage: Empty

<u>**ACTION:**</u> Clown enters stage and places hat on table. He shows the audience his top hat...turns it so they can see that it is 'empty'. He shows the audience that he has three bandannas...and explains that he will tie them together...say some magic words...and magically the scarves will untie themselves while inside the hat.

He then ties the three scarves together on diagonal corners. He shows that they are tied really tight...and pulls on them. He then rolls the three scarves together and places them into the hat.

Next he begins the 'magic' movements...hands over the top hat...magic words...etc. Slowly he reaches into the hat and removes one of the bandannas...totally untied from the others. He turns to the audience for applause. He waves his hands again and enters the hat to remove another separated bandanna. Finally, he removes the third colored bandanna from the hat. He takes his bow and accepts applause from the audience.

After his bows, he takes his hat and begins to place it on his head. In doing so, the three <u>knotted</u> scarves fall out. Embarrassed clown exits stage quickly with the knotted scarves streaming out behind him.

PREPARATION: Make a false bottom for the hat...perhaps black or the same color as the inside of the hat. The three 'untied' scarves are concealed under this false bottom of the hat.

Standing on the Cup

Number of Clowns:	One
Characters:	Generic Clown
Costumes:	Normal Wardrobe
Props:	Three styrofoam cups, all the same size. One is filled with Plaster of Paris
Stage:	Empty

<u>ACTION</u>: Clown enters stage and introduces self to audience. He mentions that he has an ordinary styrofoam cup, and that he will do something amazing right here in _____ (local town).

He says, "I'll do something right here tonight, that has never been done here in _____. I'll stand on this ordinary styrofoam cup…without crushing it. But…I'll need your help. Simply suspend all disbelief…and accept the fact that I, an ordinary clown, can stand on this ordinary cup without crushing it. Think in your mind…positive thinking…that it <u>can</u> be done."

Calls for music: MUSIC: <u>IT'S IMPOSSIBLE</u> or
                                        <u>IMPOSSIBLE DREAM.</u>

Clown discredits music…and says he will still do it. "History will be made this day right here in _____.
Do you believe? Let me hear you say YEH!!!"

Waits for audience to respond.

"Do you really believe? Let me hear you say...OK!!"

Waits for audience reaction.

Places cup on floor. Gets ready. Takes deep breath. Stands on cup and crushes it. Says, "Someone didn't believe"...and picks up cup and leaves stage.

Later in the show

Clown returns. "Boys and Girls...Ladies and Gentlemen...I have here this ordinary styrofoam cup. I've been doing a lot of homework into the art of standing on styrofoam cups. I have discovered that it's not enough to just have the boys and girls believe. It is very important that parents and grandparents also believe. Can I have some 'believable' music please?"

MUSIC: <u>IT'S IMPOSSIBLE, etc.</u>

Clown discredits music...and says he is now ready. Gets ready and approaches cup.
"Do you believe that I can stand on this cup? Say OKAY!"

Waits for audience response.

"If you really believe...say I Believe"

Waits again for audience.

Approaches cup and stands on it...the cup is crushed. He says..."Almost"...picks up cup and leaves with it.

Later in the show

Clown appears back on the stage with a new cup (this is the 'filled' cup)

Music is playing 'HIGH HOPES'

Clown says, "This time...history will be made right here in _____. Can I have the music up a little? "

MUSIC changes to IT'S IMPOSSIBLE'

Clown, "No, not that music." (music stops)

"Okay, here we go. (to audience) Let me hear you say, OKAY"

Audience reaction.

"Let me hear you say...ALL RIGHT"

Audience reaction.

Takes a deep breath and approaches cup. Gingerly places foot on cup. Lifts body upward and actually does stand on (filled) cup.

"We did it. Right here in _____. The first time in America. Thank you all for believing it could be done. We did it together".

Takes audience applause...picks up cup and leaves stage.

Walk Arounds

Christmas Cheer

Clown enters carrying box wrapped with Christmas paper. Explains that he/she is trying to get everyone into the Holiday spirit by buying this box of Christmas Cheer. He opens the box and removes some miscellaneous things like tinsel, tree bulbs, lights, etc. He then explains that he couldn't find anything really nice for the season. He then looks into the box and exclaims that Santa must have done something magical. The box is filled with Christmas cheer. He asks the audience if they would like to see it. When they say "Yes"…he reaches into the box and removes a box of CHEER Laundry Detergent…with a Christmas bow on it.

Bird Tree

Clown carries fake tree with many 'bird' symbols on it. They represent the following:

Baltimore Oreos	Nest with giant Oreo cookies and several smaller ones.
Jail Bird	Black/white stripped stuffed bird with ball and chain on leg.
Blue Jay	Letter J painted blue
Crane	Toy Crane
Stool Pigeon	A stool glued to a bird perch

Toucan   Two cans (tomato paste) fastened to a perch

Bird Dog ("Fly Do")   Stuffed dog on a perch

Your imagination can add many more to the above suggestions.

Dove - Soap

Skits for Two Clowns

COTTON CANDY

Number of Clowns: Two

Characters: Cotton Candy Salesman
Customer (clown B)

Costumes: Candy butcher wears apron and hat. Other clown is in normal clown wardrobe.

Props: Cotton Candy tray, six cotton candy cones.

Stage: Empty

ACTION: Candy salesman enters with tray full of cotton candy cones. He is holding one of the cones high in the air trying to 'sell' it to the crowd. Another clown is nearby.

Option #1

As salesman passes, Clown B, who has been using a feather duster, reaches out, behind salesman's back, and switches the cotton candy in the salesman's hand, for the feather duster that clown B is carrying. Salesman continues trying to sell the 'cotton candy', but is actually holding up the feather duster. When he finally notices the switch that has taken place, he goes over to clown B to retrieve his cotton candy. B is holding it, about to take a bite, when the salesman reaches out, takes a grasp of one end of the cotton candy, and pulls it totally off the cone leaving B holding the empty stick.

Salesman then stuffs the cotton candy into his apron, and proceeds to try to sell the remaining candy further along the parade route, circus track, or other performing area. B approaches again and repeats the previous action.

Option #2

Clown B approaches salesman to purchase one of the cotton candy cones. Money is exchanged between the two, and salesman hands one of the cones to B. As clown B walks away, salesman reaches out and grabs one end of the cotton candy. It unspools from the cone as B walks away. B finally realizes that he has been tricked and chases salesman from the area.

NOTE: If this is used as a parade or circus walk-around...all 6 pieces of cotton candy in the try can be used. Therefore allowing the gag to be performed six times before a 'reload' is necessary.

After each 'trick' Clown B hands the empty cones to the salesman (down the road a bit from the spot of the gag). Salesman stores them in his apron.

Prop construction notes:

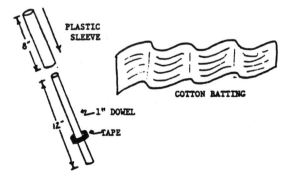

Cut piece of 1" dowel to a length of 12". Wrap tape around dowel about 3" from the bottom to increase the diameter by about ½". Cut plastic piece (actually plastic covering used for placing over a shower rod in a bathroom) to about 3" length. This plastic slips over the top portion of the dowel. Wrap cotton batting abound the plastic to look like cotton candy. Make tray for carrying the cones of candy. To make cotton candy, dye regular cotton batting to a pink color.

Disappearing Water

Number of Clowns: Two

Characters: Magician, Assistant

Costumes: Normal Wardrobe or Magician with cape

Props: Small table, pitcher of water, Plastic glass, magic wand

Stage: Empty

ACTION: Magician enters carrying magic wand, and explains to audience that he is going to perform an amazing magic trick that he's sure they have never seen before. He will make a glass of water disappear, <u>without</u> drinking it.

He calls for his assistant to bring the special props onto the stage. Assistant enters carrying tray with pitcher of water and glass. Tray is set near the center of stage, and assistant steps back to watch the trick.

Magician proceeds to partially fill glass with water, showing the audience that he is actually pouring the water into the glass. He sets the glass of water on the table and then steps in front of the table to explain to the audience just what is going to happen. He states that he will say the magic words, "Hocus Pocus...Golly Gee Whiz...I wonder where the water is". He says he will then wave his magic wand over the glass and the water will magically disappear. While he is saying all of this to the audience, the assistant picks up the glass from the table, drinks the water, and replaces the empty glass on the table.

Magician returns to the back of the table, prepared to do the trick. He starts to say "Hocus Pocus...Golly..." and notices the glass is empty. He looks bewildered...thinking that he previously poured the water into the glass...but not really sure that he did it.

He tells audience that maybe he forgot to pour the water...so "We'll try it again." He again pours the water into the glass, and steps in front of the table. He goes through the same explanation of the magic words and procedures. While he is doing this, assistant again drinks the water, but this time replaces the glass upside down on the table.

Magician returns to the back of the table and starts the magic words only to again be surprised to see the water is 'missing'. He looks suspiciously at assistant and asks if he/she had anything to do with the missing water. Assistant claims innocence and magician reluctantly picks up the glass again to pour the water.

He does not notice that the glass is upside down, and as he pours the water it runs all over the outside of the glass. He jumps back, looks suspiciously at assistant, turns the glass right side up and fills it again.

He tells assistant to "Stand way over there, so you can't mess with my water." Assistant moves a little farther from the table.

Magician again steps in front of table and explains magic words and procedures. Assistant takes glass from table and drinks the water. **BUT**…this time the assistant <u>does not swallow</u> the water. Magician returns to the table. Starts the trick and again notices the water is gone. He goes to assistant and accuses him/her of taking the water. Assistant shakes head 'no' and magician asks audience if the assistant took the water. (Audience may say yes or no depending on the crowd). In either case, magician is sure assistant took the water and demands "You took my water. I'm sure you did it. You probably did it before, too. I want my water back. Give me my water. I want the water back RIGHT NOW!"

At this point assistant sprays water on the magician. He is upset…looks at assistant…picks up table with props and chases assistant off the stage.

Dog and Hoop

Number of Clowns: Two

Characters: Animal trainer, assistant

Costumes: Animal Trainer, Normal Wardrobe

Props: Large hula hoop, stuffed dog

Stage: Empty

<u>ACTION:</u> Animal trainer enters carrying dog. He explains that he is a great animal trainer and that his pet dog is one of the best trained dogs in the world. He tells that the dog will amaze the audience with his tricks.

Clown places dog on floor and commands the dog to "Sit". Dog sits there...and clown turns to audience for applause.

He then commands the dog to "Stay" and dog does nothing. Trainer again turns to audience for applause.

Next, trainer asks dog to "Lay". Dog does nothing. Trainer again commands "Lay" (at this time he slightly moves his foot knocking the dog over), and dog lays on its side. Trainer turns to audience for applause.

Clown then says that dog will now jump through the hoop. He calls his assistant onto the stage to hold the hoop, and instructs assistant where to hold the hoop. He places the dog on the floor about 8 feet from the hoop...which is being held about 2 or 3 feet above the floor.

Trainer tells dog to "Hoop" but dog just sits there. Trainer explains to audience that perhaps the dog didn't understand the command. Trainer gets closer to dog and explains to dog that "we're gonna do the hoop trick". Assistant holds the hoop and trainer again commands the dog to "Hoop". Nothing happens.

Trainer states that maybe the dog didn't really understand him very well so he again commands the dog to "Hoop". Dog just sits there.

Trainer, getting frustrated and a bit embarrassed, goes to back of dog, gets down on hands and knees and talks into dog's ear...explaining to dog what he is supposed to do. Trainer points to the hoop and gestures that dog is supposed to jump through it. He then stands behind the dog and yells "Hoop". Dog sits there. Trainer again yells "Hoop". Dog sits. Trainer yells a third time "Hoop" and at the same time brings his foot forward to propel (kick) the dog through the hoop.

When dog flies through hoop, assistant retrieves dog...and trainer and assistant take bows and exit.

Hamburger Stand

Number of Clowns: Two

Characters: Chef (Clown B),
Generic Clown (Clown A)

Costumes: Chef's apron and hat,
Normal Clown Wardrobe

Props: Foam props: hamburger, lettuce, pickle, Swiss cheese, tomato, onion rings, flat hamburger bun with footprints on it, chef's apron and hat, small table, table top with table cloth and vase attached to bottom side of it.

Stage: Small table near center

ACTION: Clown A enters stage, "I can't find it. I've been looking everywhere. I just can't find it. I've been looking everywhere. (looks at audience) Oh, hello. Hey, have you seen the hamburger stand? I've been looking everywhere and I can't find it. I looked over here (goes to side of stage) and I can't find it. I looked way over there (other side of stage) and I can't find it. I looked way out there (looks out over audience) and I can't find it. I even looked over here and...(Clown B enters wearing chef's had and apron).

Clown A: Why, hello there. I've been looking for the hamburger stand and I can't find it. It used to be right here. Did you see it?

Clown B: Well sure. It's still here.

Clown A: Right here? It doesn't look like it did last year.

Clown B: No? Well what did it look like?

Clown A: Well, last year it was really neat. It had a table cloth, and flowers, and all kinds of nice things.

Clown B: Still does. (Flips table-top over revealing vase and table-cloth)

Clown A: Now that's the hamburger stand I remember. (to audience), Ya' know, there are two very special things I really like about this hamburger stand.
The first thing is that no matter how many times you've been here, he remembers exactly how you like your burger. Even if you've only been here one time, and come back a year later, he still remembers exactly how you like it. He never forgets.

Clown B: I never forget.

Clown A: And the second thing I like is…if you're in a hurry…this is the place to be…because he's FAST

Clown B: I'm FAST.

Clown A: Hey Chef. Would you do me a favor?

Clown B: What's that? What do you want me to do?

Clown A: Would you make me a hamburger?

Clown B: Sure. I'd love to make you a hamburger.

Clown A: Make it right away?

Clown B: Sure. How do you want it?

Clown A: Just like I always have it. C'mon, you remember. (to audience) He never forgets.

Clown B: Oh yeah. I never forget.

Clown A: I'll tell you what. I'm going to tell <u>them</u> exactly how I like it…while you go back there and make the burger.

Clown B: OK. I won't listen to you. You just tell them. (Clown B <u>does</u> listen to hear what A is saying)

Clown A: (to audience) He starts off with a big old hamburger bun.. about this big around (shows with hands). Then he puts on that thick juicy hamburger. I can hear it cooking now. He puts on that top bun, and brings it over to you. (Clown B comes back carrying burger on bun) …on a nice crispy bed of lettuce. I love lettuce. That's my favorite. I love it.

Clown B: (Realizes he doesn't have lettuce on it.)…A nice crispy bed of what?

Clown A: A bed of lettuce. Is that my hamburger?

Clown B: NOOOO. Yours has a nice crispy bed of lettuce…remember?

Clown A: Yeah, now I remember. He never forgets.

Clown B: I never forget.

Clown A: Amazing...and he's fast, too.

Clown B: Yeah. I'm fast.

Clown A: (to audience) He starts off with a big ol' bun about this big around. Puts on a crispy bed of lettuce. Puts on that big juicy hamburger   ...puts it right on top...and puts on the bun.
Then he brings it over to you. (Clown B is bringing it out) ....with a nice piece of melted Swiss cheese on it. I love Swiss cheese.

Clown B: (realizes that burger does not have cheese on it.

Clown B: Hey _____. A nice piece of melted   Swiss what?

Clown A: Swiss cheese. Is that mine?

Clown B: NOOO. Yours has a piece of melted swiss cheese on it.   Remember?

Clown A: Sure I remember. He never forgets.

Clown B: I never forget.

Clown A: And he's fast.

Clown B: I'm fast.

Clown A: Well he starts off with a big ol' hamburger bun…about this big around…puts on that crispy bed of   lettuce…puts on the juicy burger…a nice piece of melted swiss cheese…and puts on that bun.
(B enters carrying the burger). Then he tops it off with a slice of round tomato. Do you like red tomatoes? I love 'em.

Clown B: Hey _____. A slice of round red what?

Clown A: Red tomato. Is that mine?

Clown B: (asking audience). Is this his? NOOOO. Yours has a nice round red tomato …remember?

Clown A: Oh yeah. Now I remember. He never forgets.

Clown B: I never forget.

Clown A And he's fast.

Clown B: I'm fast.

Clown A: He starts off with a bun about this big around. Puts on that crispy bed of lettuce…then the thick juicy hamburger. He puts on that melted slice of Swiss cheese…and then a round red tomato, and the other bun. (B enters with burger) …and   tops it off with a couple of onion rings. I love onion rings.

Clown B: A couple of what?

Clown A: Onion rings. Is that mine?

Clown B: (to audience) Is this his? NOOOO. Yours has onion rings…remember?

Clown A: I remember. He never forgets.

Clown B: I never forget.

Clown A: And he's fast.

Clown B: I'm fast.

Clown A: He starts off with a big ol' hamburger bun…puts on that crispy bed of lettuce…and that big juicy hamburger patty. Next he adds the melted Swiss cheese and a nice round red tomato…a couple of onion rings…and brings it over to me (B enters with burger)…topped off with a nice piece of pickle.

Clown B: A little piece of what?

Clown A: A piece of pickle. Is that mine?

Clown B: Is this his? NOOOOOO. Yours has a nice of pickle….remember?

Clown A: Now I remember. He never forgets.

Clown B: I never forget.

Clown A: And he's fast.

Clown B: I'm fast.

Clown A: Anyway...I'm kind of in a hurry. Would you do me a favor?

Clown B: (shakes head agreeably...but is tired)

Clown A: Would you put a pickle on top of that?...and step on it...I'm in a hurry.

Clown B: Put the pickle on top? And step on it?

Clown A: Yeah. I'm really in a hurry. (to audience) He's going to put the pickle on it for me, and then I'll be all set. He starts off with the big ol' hamburger....

Clown B: (interrupting) Hey _____. You want me to put a pickle on top?

Clown A: Put the pickle on top...and step on it. I'm in a hurry.

Clown B: Hey _____. Are you sure?

Clown A: (to audience) What did I ask him to do? (they respond). And what do I want him to do? (they respond). That's not so difficult.

Clown B: (Smashing the burger and jumping on it while singing) Special orders don't upset us...(brings out the burger with footprints on top of it)

Clown A: Hey, _____. What's that?

Clown B: You told me to STEP ON IT.

Clown A: I'm gonna get you.

Clown B: No you're not.

Clown A: I won't? Why not?

Clown B: Cause I'm fast.

      A chases B off of stage.

Special Note: Every time clown A is describing how B makes the burger…Clown B is on the side of the stage actually doing each step that A mentions. B then proceeds toward A with burger (which is incomplete). B stops short of A and pulls burger back when he tells A that it is not A's burger and B returns to the table to add additional items to it.

Have a Seat

Number of Clowns:	Two
Characters:	Generic Clowns (A & B)
Costumes:	Normal Wardrobe
Props:	Bench and Hat. Long Shirt
Stage:	Bench on stage.

ACTION: Clown A enters stage and takes a seat on the bench. He places his hat on the remaining part of the bench. Clown B enters stage, wearing a large jacket, and the long shirt. He attempts to sit on the bench. Clown A says, "You can't sit there." Clown B asks, "Why not?" Clown A, "Because my hat is there. You'll crush it. There's no room for you to sit down."

Clown B tries, many times, to trick clown A into moving the hat and making room, but Clown A is usually too fast to allow space for B to sit down. Clown A picks up the hat,...picks something off of it...looks at it, etc...and B tries to sit each time, but Clown A always manages to get his hat back on the bench before B can sit down.

Finally Clown B goes into the audience and talks with people. He meets someone and says, "You didn't tell me you were coming. This is really great. I'm really glad to see you." Clown B calls to Clown A (who is sitting on the bench), "_____. You won't believe who's here. He's so excited to see you. He has a special present for you. A chocolate cake. Come on down here and get it."

Clown A...suspiciously leave bench and makes his way toward the audience. When he nears audience member...Clown B runs past...and onto the stage to take a seat on the bench.

Clown A discovers there was no cake in the audience and returns to the stage to confront Clown B. they are both mad...and B gets up...and removes coat. They do the long shirt routine...and when B's pants fall down...they chase off of the stage.

High Diver

Number of Clowns: Two

Characters;   Diver (clown A), Assistant (Clown B)

Costumes: Diving costume, (fins, bathing cap, and swimsuit)

Props: Four foot ladder, three buckets, (one with water, one w/ popcorn, one empty)

Stage: One bucket (popcorn) is on one side of the stage.

ACTION: Clown A (diver) enters as the great high-diver...followed by Clown B, his dumb assistant who is carrying the ladder and two buckets (water, empty)

Clown A announces that he plans a great high-dive from an enormous height into the bucket of water. He gestures to his assistant to set up the water bucket at the bottom of the ladder.

After much difficulty, the assistant sets up the ladder and places the empty bucket at the bottom. He pours water from the other bucket into the empty one. With much hoopla, the diver climbs the ladder and stands on the very top. (BE CAREFUL WITH THIS) He puts his hands in front of himself indicating he is ready to dive...but stops. He motions for the assistant to add more water into the bucket. Assistant does so.

Diver is again ready to dive...but assistant tells him to wait. Clown B indicates that diver should do a somersault type of dive. The diver is not prepared to do that and indicates that he is too scared for that dive. Clown B then indicates that he should turn around and do a BACKWARD dive into the bucket.

With much difficulty, the diver turns around with his back to the bucket, and prepares to dive. Meanwhile, the assistant moves the water bucket about 10 feet back from the ladder.

Clown A prepares to dive, puts his feet on the side rails of the ladder, and SLIDES down the rails...doing a backward somersault when he reaches the floor. He gets up...looking for the bucket he 'missed.' He sees that it was been moved, and demands that assistant bring the bucket over to him. While attempting to do that, assistant 'trips' and throws the water on the diver.

The diver, now really mad, looks around, spots the third bucket (popcorn) and chases the assistant into the audience. He proceeds to throw the contents of the bucket on the assistant and audience...and they chase each other off.

PROP SETUP:

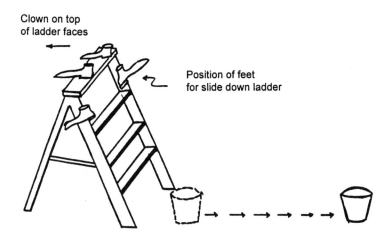

Clown on top of ladder faces ←

Position of feet for slide down ladder

JUST ONE HAND

Number of Clowns:	Two
Characters:	Normal Clowns
Costumes:	Normal Wardrobe
Props:	1 glass of water, 1 saucer, 1 table
Stage:	Stage is set near center of stage

ACTION: Clown A is on stage, having just finished a bit of business. Clown B enters carrying a glass of water on a saucer. B says the management has sent this special glass of water for Clown A because he/she has been working so hard and might be thirsty.

Clown A reaches for the water, but B stops A...saying there is one stipulation. The glass must be held with "**Just One Hand**". Clown a steps back...looks at the water and says, "I can drink it with just one hand"...while reaching for the water. Clown B again holds the water our of A's reach and says there's one more stipulation. Clown B says he/she must place the water on the table, first, then A can drink it. Clown A agrees to that. Clown B says, further, that A must close his/her eyes while B is putting the water on the table. Clown A is somewhat suspicious, but agrees.

When Clown A has eyes closed, B takes saucer from under the water and puts it on **TOP** of the glass. Clown B then inverts the glass and saucer, with the glass now sitting upside down on the saucer, and the water 'trapped' inside the glass. B puts the saucer on the table, then tells Clown a to open his eyes.

Clown A opens his eyes and begins to reach for the water, but stops when seeing that the water will spill all over if the glass is picked up. Clown A tells Clown B that he/she isn't really thirsty, and probably doesn't want the water. Clown B encourages A to try it. A looks at the glass, and tries to figure out a way to pick it up, but gives up. Clown B asks A if it is OK if he drinks the water. Clown A agrees but makes the same rule, that B must do it with **Just One Hand.** Clown B says "No Problem". B picks up the saucer (with the glass on top of it), tilts his head way back, and places the saucer on his forehead. He then takes his hand off the saucer, and places it on the glass...holding the glass tight to the saucer. He leans forward until the glass is upright and the saucer is on top of it.

He then places both the saucer and the glass on the table. He is proud of his accomplishments.

Clown B then turns to the audience and says, "Now, I'll remove the saucer from the glass...with **Just One Hand.**" He takes the saucer off and moves away from the table to show it to the audience.

While Clown B is in front of the table, Clown A picks up the glass and begins to drink the water.

Clown B, not aware of A's actions, turns back to get the glass, and starts to say, "Now I'll drink the wa....". He sees Clown A drinking it and asks A what he is doing. Clown A says, "I'm drinking the water with **Just One Hand**.

Clown B chases Clown A off of the stage.

On A Date

Number of Clowns:	Two
Characters:	Boy Clown and Girl Clown
Costumes:	Appropriate for characters
Props:	Signs: "Her Home", "Traffic Jam", "Lovers Lane", "Book of "Instructions", Car Horn, 2 Chairs, Flowers
Stage:	Two chairs facing audience.

ACTION: Boy clown enters carrying flowers. He goes to chairs, and 'enters' drivers side door. (Chairs represent the front seats of a car). He puts flowers on passenger seat and starts engine. He starts jiggling, simulating that he is riding in the moving car. He clutches, brakes, shifts, signals with arm, etc. as if driving car. He checks for address (have slip of paper in pocket). Finally he brakes, stops jiggling, and gets out of car. He goes around the back of the car...to passenger door, opens it, removes flowers, and shuts door.

He goes to house (at the edge of the stage with "Her Home" sign). He gulps and acts nervous. He knocks on the door. It opens and girl clown appears. He gives her the flowers, offers his arm, and leads her to the car. He opens the passenger side door, and she awkwardly gets in and sits. He closes the door, goes around the back of the car, and enters the drivers side.

Girl looks straight ahead, dead-pan. Boy starts car, and both start jiggling. He clutches, brakes, signals, etc. They come to one big traffic jam. He reaches out of 'window' and stands up sign ("Traffic Jam") that was laying there.

He honks repeatedly (girl has car horn under her costume and she blows horn when he pretends to hit car horn). Girl urges him to go and 'speak' to the driver of the car ahead of him. He finally turns off his engine, gets out of his door, goes to stage front, and starts 'talking' to the driver of a small car ahead of his. He kicks the tires, hits the car top, offers to trade punches, eggs driver on…then steps aside in a fighting stance while the 'other' (imaginary) driver gets out.

Boys eyes and head visibly move upward as the 'big' driver stands up. Boy drops fighting stance, dusts off other driver and goes back to his own car, opens door, sits down, and starts engine. They jiggle again. He clutches, brakes, signals, etc. as they begin to 'move forward'.

Boy reaches out and turns sign around so audience can see back of sign which reads "Lovers Lane".

Car stutters to a stop (they bounce and come to a stop). He tries to start engine with no luck. He looks at her. She urges him to check the engine. He reluctantly gets out, opens hood and looks in. Scratches his head. Goes to side of car, still looking under the hood. Still a mystery. He 'slams' the hood closed and gets back into the car. He explains to the girl that they are 'stuck'. She doesn't believe him, and hands him the 'Instruction Book" (which was under her car seat). He studies instructions, stretching while reading the book and letting his arm go on the back of her seat and around her. She hits him with the flowers. He studies again...then tries to kiss her. She hits him again. He studies the book some more. "Sees" reference to the shift lever in the book. He reaches for it and 'accidentally' grabs her knee. She hits him again. He is now really upset. He puts the instruction book down and is able to start the car (they jiggle). He shifts, clutches, brakes, etc...and they drive back to her 'home'.

He stops the car (they stop jiggling). He gets out of his door...goes around the back of car to her door, opens it and pulls her out. He slams the door and walks her to her house then turns around to leave. She taps him on the shoulder and whistles at him. He turns back. She kisses him a nice juicy, audible kiss. He reacts...jumps, kicks heels, and shouts 'wow', grabs her hand and they both run off the stage together.

Paint Company

Number of Clowns:	Two
Characters;	Boss Painter (A), Painter (B)
Costumes:	Coveralls (perhaps covered with paint)
Props:	Easel, Sign, 5 buckets, Soap (for paint), Tarp, Ladder, Brushes, Whistle
Stage:	Empty

<u>ACTION</u>: Boss Clown (A) enters stage with sign "Ace Painting Company" painted on one side. Other side says "We're Number One". Clown A puts sign on Easel.

Boss clown blows whistle and motions for Clown B (painter) to come on stage. A leaves stage and goes around so that he is behind B when B enters. B enters stage very slowly...acting shy and carrying ladder. He is looking for the Boss Painter.

Clown A, standing behind B, taps B on the back. B turns around, swinging the ladder, and ladder knocks A down. Clown B, seeing A on the ground, turns back to his original position. A again taps B on the back, but DUCKS quickly before B can spin the ladder. B turns around with ladder going over A's head. A gets up. B turns back with ladder, hitting A again on the back and again knocking him down.

Clown A gets up...hits B...and tells him where to set up the ladder. Clown B sets up the ladder in the center of the stage, and leaves the stage to get bucket(s) of paint. While B is gone, A spreads a drop cloth on the stage. Clown B walks in backward while carrying buckets (as if looking at someone in the wings)...and knocks A down and falls on him. Clown a gets up...yells at B...and tells him to get some more paint, and put it on the ladder. Clown B gets a bucket of paint and sets it on top of the ladder.

Clown B gets another bucket from the other side of the stage, and puts that on top of ladder, too. He then reports to A that everything is ready. A tells B to go get the brushes. B walks under the ladder...pulling on a hanging fish line...and tips one of the buckets off (spilling the paint.) Clown A tells B to never walk under a ladder. It's bad luck. B concurs, but doesn't really believe him. B goes back under the ladder the other way...to get roller...and other bucket is pulled down on him.

Clown A says they need more paint...and B goes to get more paint. This time B climbs the ladder. When he gets to the top...he teeters...and drops the bucket on his boss. Clown a stands there counting to ten...and realizing what happened. Clown B comes down the ladder to check on A...who still has the bucket on his head.

A removes the bucket...and chases B off the stage.

Painters

Number of Clowns: Two

Characters: Boss Painter (A), and Painter (B)

Costumes: Painter clothes, one pair of tear-away pants.

Props: 2 large buckets, 2 paint buckets, 1 Roll of wallpaper (vinyl), Clipboard, 4 foam brushes.

Stage;   2 Buckets with 'wallpaper paste', board across two chairs to serve as table (or actual table), chair.

ACTION: Clown A enters (carrying clipboard and wallpaper), leading clown B (carrying two buckets of paint). They walk on stage with A looking around surveying the situation, while B is 'skylarking'. A suddenly stops and B continues walking into the back of A...pushing him forward causing A to drop wallpaper and clipboard.

A: Comes back and pushes B
B: Drops buckets (actually <u>places</u> buckets down hard on floor) with one landing on A's toe.
A: Reacts. Slaps B. B spins around and falls.
B: Gets up...as A is reaching down for clipboard he dropped when B first pushed him. B Kicks A.
A: Falls forward from kick.
B: Picks up paint buckets and steps back.
A: Takes paintbrush from B's bucket...and paints B's shirt.

B: Sets buckets down, then throws paint on A (flicking brush)
A: Throws paint on B (flicking brush)
Then bends down to pick up clipboard.
B: Hits A on the butt with paintbrush
A: (after doing forward roll) gets up, takes brush, and paints all of B's clothing.
Then A says "Let's get to work" and takes wallpaper roll and begins to unroll it on table, while B is getting paste ready to apply to the back of wallpaper.
B: Takes brush with paste and holds it high in the air. As B brings brush down toward wallpaper...A pulls paper off table and brush hits empty table. B looks surprised.
A: Laughs and puts paper back on table for another try of applying paste.
B: As before, B lifts brush to bring it down on paper. As he does so...A again pulls paper off table before B can apply paste. B again looks surprised and confused.
A: Laughing, puts paper back on table for a third try.
B: Lifts brush again with paste, but instead of lowering it to apply paste to paper, B swings the brush toward A, hitting him in the chest with the paste brush.
A: Is mad...but says..."Let's get this paper up. You get on the chair and take this paper with you."
B: Picks up paste bucket, holding it on his shoulder, with wallpaper in other hand. He climbs up onto the chair (using it like a ladder). As he climbs, he spills the paint backward onto Clown A who is standing behind him.
B then comes down, laughs, and checks out the wallpaper.

A: Gets another bucket of paste and puts it over B's head.
B: Turns around and, in turning, gets wallpaper wrapped around himself.
A: Takes one end of wallpaper and pulls it, spinning B around and getting out of the wallpaper. (Talking to B) "Now let's get some painting done" and he goes across stage to begin pretending to paint an imaginary wall.
B: Comes up behind A and pulls A by the belt, indicating that he wants A to come over to his side.
A: Annoyed, slaps B's hand from his belt and continues trying to paint 'his' wall.
B: Comes up behind A again, and grabs the belt to get A to come over to B's side.
A: More annoyed, again removes B's hand from the belt and tells B to go paint.
B: Starts to cross stage but changes his mind and again tugs on A's belt to try to get A to join him in the painting.
A: Is really annoyed and tells B to go away.
B: Finally accepting the fact that A will not help, waves at A and crosses stage to begin painting "his" wall.
A: Calls to B to 'come over here and paint'.
B: Motions that A should 'get lost' and returns to painting his own wall.
A: Crosses stage to B, plans to pulls B's belt this time to get B to come over to help him. When A tugs on B's pants, they 'break-away' and B is left standing there in his clown underwear.
B: Notices his situation…looks around to see A holding the pants…and chases A from the stage.

Pizza Man

Number of Clowns:	Two
Characters:	Pizza Salesman (A), Prospective customer (B).
Costumes:	Salesman wears chef's hat and apron, Other clown has normal clown wardrobe.
Props:	Foam Pizza w/ elastic connected to one slice.
Stage:	Empty

ACTION: Pizza salesman enters carrying foam pizza and gesturing to audience that it certainly smells good. He asks, "Who ordered this wonderful pizza?"...while looking around the audience to see if anyone responds. He does this for several seconds...looking at various people in the audience and asking "Is this your pizza?"

Clown B enters, comes up to salesman and says, "I'll have some."

Salesman does not want to give pizza to B, and tells him "NO. This pizza is for someone else."

Salesman again proceeds to ask audience if anyone ordered this tasty pizza. (More looks around the audience). Clown B again approaches asking for a piece of the pizza. Salesman again tells him to 'go away', and tries to sell the pizza to someone in the audience.

Clown B approaches, for a third time, asking for a taste of the pizza. Salesman finally relents and offers B a slice of the pizza. B is satisfied, hungry, and now...happy. He takes the piece of pizza and starts to walk away...only to notice that the 'cheese' (elastic cord) is still attached to the rest of the pie. Salesman and Clown B struggle to separate the piece from the rest of the pie, stretching the elastic back and forth. Finally B lets go of the piece of pizza. It flies back to A and knocks him down. At this time he tosses the entire pizza into the air. Salesman gets up and chases B off the stage, or out of the arena.

For a parade, or walk-around gag, pizza can be restored and gag is repeated at another location.

PIZZA CONSTSUCTION NOTES:

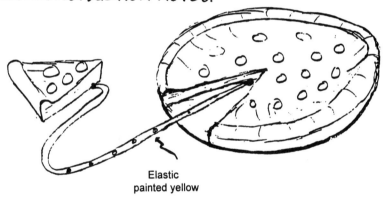

Elastic
painted yellow

Cut 20-24 inch circle from 2 inch thick foam. Cut 20-24" circle from 3/8 FOAM CORE, heavy cardboard, or plywood for base of pizza (pizza pan). Cut, shape, and paint the pizza to look real. Add 'pepperoni' pieces. Glue them on with contact cement. Cut <u>slice</u> from pizza, (using electric knife). Paint tray silver. Attach 6 foot piece of ¼" elastic to both center of tray and slice of pizza.

Be sure the elastic is painted yellow prior to installing it.
Glue pizza to tray. **Do not glue pizza 'slice' to tray.** The slice will just sit on the tray during the execution of the skit.

Right Toe

Number of Clowns: Two

Characters: Normal Clowns (A & B)

Costumes: Normal Wardrobe

Props: None

Stage: Empty

<u>ACTION:</u> Clown A enters stage to greet audience. Clown B enters and comes up next to Clown A. Clown B stands with his foot on top of A's right toe. They begin talking to each other.

B: Do you see that fine audience out there?
A: Right Toe.
B: This is one of the finest audiences I've ever seen.
A: Right Toe
B: Do you think we're going to have fun today?
A: Right Toe
B: Hasn't our weather been beautiful, lately?
A: Right Toe
B: What's the matter with you? Every time I ask you a question, you say "Right Toe".
A: That's because you're standing on my Right Toe.
B: Looks down...sees the problem...and they either chase off or A tells B to leave.

Sharpshooter

Number of Clowns: Two

Characters: Sharpshooter (A), Target Holder (B)

Costumes: Western type (shooter)
Normal Wardrobe (holder)

Props: Starter Pistol, Target, Four Balloons, Record, "Bang" gun, Two Crackers, Mouse Trap, Mirror, Small Table

Stage: Empty

ACTION: Sharpshooter enters with target in hand, searching for an assistant. He asks audience for volunteer (disregarding anyone in audience), and notices that Clown B has entered stage. B is engaged by sharpshooter and asked to hold the target. He is unwilling, but A 'convinces' him to be the assistant. B is given the target to hold, as A paces off 10 steps across the stage to his shooting position. B paces directly behind A as they cross the stage.

When A reaches the end of his walk...he turns, quickly, and fires the gun. As he turns, B ducks...and A fires directly over his head...not knowing that B was directly behind him. A is upset that no one is holding the target.

He returns B to the proper target position...and this time gives him two balloons to hold. One balloon is positioned high in the air (B holds his arm above his head with balloon), and the other balloon is low at B's side. A returns to his firing position.

He takes aim at the target balloon in the air and fires. The OTHER balloon breaks. (B actually breaks it by squeezing it with his hand).

A is upset at his inability to hit the correct target. (You can use a third clown here as an announcer if you desire.) If you use a third clown, A asks him to hold a 45 rpm phonograph record between him and the target. A will now shoot at the balloon by firing the bullet through the record and then hitting the balloon. He completes this successfully. (B actually broke the balloon when A fired.) A takes appropriate bows.

Now A hands B a cracker to hold, and announces that he will break it by hitting it with a bullet. While A returns to his shooting position, B begins eating the cracker. Clown A turns around and sees this. He goes back to B and straightens him out…gives another cracker and returns to fire. B holds the cracker in the air. A fires…'hits' cracker…and it shatters***

Finally A gives B the remaining two balloons to hold…one on each side of his head. A takes a mirror and faces away from B. He looks into the mirror to aim…shoots…and "breaks" both balloons at the same time…with the same bullet.

While A is taking appropriate bows…B is looking at remaining props on the table. B finds another gun (the BANG gun, which is actually a gun that opens when fired and displays a small flag that hangs down with the word 'Bang' on it). He aims it at A while A is bowing.

A turns around...sees B...and is annoyed about being 'upstaged'. He turns...B fires 'BANG' gun...and sign is displayed. A is more upset. He aims his gun at B and fires. B's pants fall down...and A chases B off of stage.

***NOTE: When B holds cracker, he conceals a small mousetrap in his hand with the 'snapper' held down, and cracker held up on platform of trap. When A fires, B lets the trap release, and 'snapper' breaks cracker. Practice this carefully to be sure your fingers are out of the way.

Stagecoach

Number of Clowns: Two

Characters: Cowboys (Stagecoach Driver and Shotgun Person)

Costumes: Bandannas and cowboy hats

Props: Two chairs, guns and whip for cowboys.

Stage: Two chairs in center

ACTION: The two 'Clownboys' enter the stage with one the driver of the 'stagecoach' and the other will be riding shotgun. The driver invites the other to "Have a seat on the old stagecoach...we've gotta ride'.

They both take seats and driver appears to hold reins as if controlling the horses. Shotgun clown takes a seat to his right. Driver cracks whip to 'start' horses moving, and he begins bouncing and weaving. Shotgun clown remains still.

Driver notices that shotgun is not bouncing, looks at him, gives him a jab to the ribs. Shotgun gets the message and begins to bounce, too.

As they drive along, Shotgun keeps looking back...and appears concerned as if someone is following then. He says, "Hey boss. There's someone riding real fast toward us. I think this means danger'.

Driver, "How big is he?" Shotgun clown, "He's about this big" (indicating with thumb and forefinger that person behind them appears to be about 3 inches high). Driver says, "No problem. He's about 3 days behind us. Keep on riding". They ride ahead some more.

Shotgun looks back again and says, "He's gaining on us." Driver asks, "How big is he now?" Shotgun says, "He's about this big" (indicating with both hands that person is about 8 inches tall). Driver, "No problem. He's still two days behind us. Keep on riding". They ride some more.

Shotgun looks back again...even more concerned...and says, "He's getting closer. He's almost here. What'r we gonna do?" Driver, "How big is he now?" Shotgun, "He's about this big" (indicates with both hands that person is about 24 inches tall). Driver, "Uh, oh. He's getting too close. You'd better shoot him." Shotgun, "What?" Driver, "Shoot him"

Shotgun takes aim...but then puts gun down and says, "I can't shoot him." Driver, "You can't shoot him? Why not?" Shotgun, "I've known him since he was this big" (indicating with thumb and finger about 3 inches tall). Driver, "Well if you can't shoot him...you may as well join him" and driver pushes shotgun off of chair onto the floor. Driver exits stage. Shotgun gets up and chases driver off.

Telephone Call

Number of Clowns:	Two
Characters:	Telephone Operator (A), Caller (B)
Costumes:	Telephone hard-hat, Normal Clown Wardrobe
Props:	Box with telephone in it, (rigged with ball on stretch cord), chair, newspaper or book
Stage:	Chair and Telephone box are on one side of the stage

ACTION: Clown A (telephone operator) enters and takes seat on chair behind telephone box. He begins to read a newspaper or book. Clown B enters looking to make a telephone call. He notices telephone and box, and begins to move toward it to make a call. He changes his mind and starts to walk away. Changes his mind again, checks pocket for money and returns to telephone box to make a call. Clown A, behind newspaper, does not see Clown B, so B tries to get his attention by waving…and moving around. Finally Clown B kicks the telephone box with a loud sound and Clown A falls backward off of the chair.

A: Gets up and asks, "What do you want?"
B: "Are you a telephone operator?"
A: Looks at hard-hat, looks at sign, and says, "Yep. Now what do you want?"
B: "I want to make a telephone call"
A: "Well you've come to the right place…but you'll need a telephone."

B: "Well, do you have one?"
A: Looks in box and says, "Yep"…then hands phone to Clown B
A: "Where to you want to call?"
B: "I want to call my gramma"
A: "Where does your gramma live?"
B: "She lives in IOWA (Eye-Oh-Way)"
A: "Where's EYE-OH-WAY?"
B: Pointing in front of him…"It's down the HIGHWAY (High-Oh-Way)"
A: "Well, that's a long distance call. You'll have to go over there to make your call."
B: Walks away from clown A…across stage and in the process he steps over the stretch cord so that is is now between his legs. He moves about ½ way across the stage so that cord is taught, but not stretched out yet. He asks, "How's that?"
A: Checking tension on cord…"That's good. Let me check your call" He looks into telephone box.

NOTE: Be sure that clown A has his <u>foot</u> or <u>chair</u> resting on the telephone box base at this point, because when cord is stretched the tension will tend to pull the box toward Clown B and it will slide across the stage.

B: "Oh, I forgot. My Gramma moved"
A: "Where'd she move to?"
B: "She moved to CALIFORNIA (Cal-If-<u>F</u>_orn_-I-AAA)"
A: "CAL-IF-<u>FORN</u>-EYE-AAA?"
B: "Yep, CAL-IF-FORN-EYE-AAA"
A: "Where's that?"
B: "<u>Farther</u> down the HIGH-OH-WAY"
A: "Farther down the HIGH-OH-WAY?"
B: "Yep, farther down the HIGH-OH-WAY"
A: "Well then, you'll have to go farther over there. That's a <u>longer</u> distance call"
B: "I just want to <u>call</u> her. I don't want to <u>walk</u> over there." He looks apprehensive, but moves farther away as cord begins to stretch and become more taught. "How's that?"
A: Checks tension...motions to audience that 'we're going to have a little fun with this clown', and says "You've got to go a little <u>farther.</u>" (A tries to get the audience to say 'farther' with him)
B: Moves reluctantly and looks back...sees cord stretching...and asks, "How's this?"
A: Again checks tension and says, "Got to go (motions to audience to join him)...a little <u>farther</u>"
B: Begins to look scared, and moves more. He asks, "Is this far enough?"
A: Checks tension again and says, "Take two more giant steps (motions for audience) <u>Farther</u>"
B: Hesitates, looks back questioningly, and moves two small or medium steps farther away. Asks, "Is this far enough?"
A: Checks tension...nods head up and down ...motions to audience to watch what's going to happen to this guy and says, "That looks pretty good. You can dial your Gramma now"

B: Looking relieved...begins dialing telephone. He says, "Hello Gramma". Doesn't get any response. Shakes telephone and says, "Hello Gramma?"
Still no response. He yells back at clown A and says, "I don't hear my Gramma"
A: Checks tension...looks at audience and says, "It looks OK here. I'll get your call for you" (winks at audience)
B: "OK. Let me have it."
A: Looks surprisingly at audience and says, "What did you say?"
B: "I said, LET ME HAVE IT"
A: Drawing out the suspense asks, "What?"
B: Getting annoyed and impatient. He is now bending over so that cord is between his legs and stretched tightly. He <u>yells</u>, **"LET ME HAVE IT"**
A: Opens top of telephone box quickly...ball flies out and hits Clown B in the butt. B falls forward, rolls, gets up and picks up the ball, telephone, and cord. He chases Clown A from the stage.

Prop Construction:

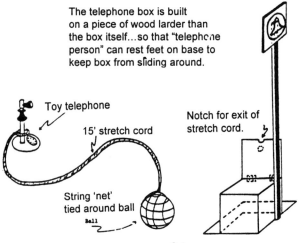

The telephone box is built on a piece of wood larder than the box itself...so that "telephone person" can rest feet on base to keep box from sliding around.

Toy telephone

15' stretch cord

Notch for exit of stretch cord.

String 'net' tied around ball

Tumblers

Number of clowns:	Two
Characters:	Tumblers
Costumes:	Tank tops, shorts, socks, tennis shoes
Props:	Tumbling mat
Stage:	Tumbling mat in center

ACTION: Two clowns enter stage and bounce around, indicating they are 'acrobatic' clowns. Perhaps they do some tumbling, clapping, stretching, etc.

After getting 'ready' Clown A claps his hands to get the attention of Clown B. Clown B acknowledges Clown A's clap, by doing a clap of his own. He looks to Clown A for instructions.

Clown A indicates to Clown B that he wants him to climb up his body to form a "Totem Pole" (two man high) effect. He indicates, by tapping various parts of his body, where he wants Clown B to step. He taps his knee, his hip, and his shoulder…indicating where B should place his feet while on the way to standing on his shoulders.

Clown B goes over to Clown A and taps the same places (on Clown A) indicating where he is to place his feet. However, Clown B taps a little harder, kind of 'punching' Clown A. A indicates his 'concern' about the intensity of the taps…but they continue on.

Clown B goes back across the stage. They look at each other, and Clown A again indicates where B is to place his feet. Clown B returns and again taps (rather hard) the spots on Clown A. A is getting a bit angry, ...but continues.

Clown B goes back across stage to get ready. Clown A takes a position to 'catch' Clown B. B makes a long run across the stage for the 'mount' but changes his mind at the last minute...and knocks Clown A over. Clown A gets up, angry, and again taps out the foot positions on his body. Clown B repeats the taps on A's body and A is about ready to start a fight with B...but holds himself back and indicates that B should go back across the stage and try again.

They repeat the run-up but this time Clown B's foot kicks Clown A in the rear and knocks him over. They now go into a big of a fight with slaps and falls...and finally agree to make up.

They stand apart with hands spread wide, right hand up, and left hand downward. They approach and each puts arms around the other two times. They get down on their knees, facing each other, and again put arms around each other twice. Clown A leans back a bit and looks to audience while B dips his head to the floor leaving his rear sticking up in the air. Clown A attempts to hug Clown again but this time ends up putting his arms around Clown B's rump. He is annoyed. Pushes Clown B over. They get up and Clown A chases Clown B from the stage.

Two on a Chair

Number of Clowns:	Two
Characters:	Generic Clowns (A & B)
Costumes:	Normal Wardrobe
Props:	Sturdy chair with straight back, Two musical instruments or kazoos
Stage:	Chair in center of stage

ACTION: Clown A enters carrying kazoo (or actual instrument). He nods to audience and indicates, or verbally tells them, he is going to play a tune. He then proceeds to sit on a chair and play a tune…such as "Be a clown". A sits with legs together.

While A is playing, Clown B enters and creates impression to audience that he does not 'see' clown A on the chair. B moves toward chair and sits on Clown A's lap, with his legs on the <u>outside</u> of A's legs. He immediately is aware that something is wrong. He looks down…counts the number of legs "1-2-3-4". Both clowns jump up, and look around rather confused.

Clown A asks, :"What do you want?" B, "I want to play a song". A, But there's only one chair…you can't play." B, "But I want to play, too". A then appears to think about it…gets an idea…and agrees. "OK, I'll fix it so we can both play."

A goes back (upstage) and turns chair on it's side…while B is excitedly talking to audience about the fact that they're both going to play a song. B, "Oh boy. He's going to let me play, too. We're going to play a duet…both of us." (Actually B is stalling for time to allow A to get the chair properly set for the gag.)

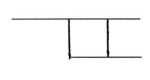

When the chair is properly set, A returns to the front of the stage and invites B to move to the chair and 'have a seat.' B must be careful to keep his eyes on the audience so as to create the impression that he does not see the chair has been turned on its side.

A takes a seat on the leg part of the chair while B is sitting over the unsupported back of the chair.

They play the "Billboard March" (or a similar fast tune, and at the end, A jumps up and runs to the front of the stage (downstage) to take a bow. When he gets up, B falls to the floor.

A is excited about how he "got him" (B). A, running back and forth near the front of the stage says something like, "I got him that time. He fell right on the floor. Did you see that?"

While A is at the front of the stage, B is upstage turning the chair around (180 degrees), so that A will now be sitting over the unsupported back of the chair. When B has the chair turned, he invites A to play a 'slow song'. A must be careful to <u>not notice</u> that the chair has been turned around. They both sit on the same sides of the stage as in the first sitting on the chair, but the chair has been turned.

They both take seats with B now sitting over the <u>leg part</u> of the chair and A sitting over the <u>unsupported</u> back.

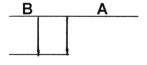

While they play (the slow tune), both get up together (shoulder to shoulder) slowly, to the surprise of the audience, which is expecting B to get up and A to fall to the floor. After this slow rise together, they both sit back down again, slowly. They then both get up again, together, and both sit again. At the end of the song, both jump up at the same time, go to the front of the stage for applause, and the chair has not tipped during this song.

NOTE: It is important to practice standing up together and sitting down together. If the two clowns are 'touching' each other at the shoulder or elbows when sitting, one clown can indicate the 'rise' move to the other by nudging the other slightly with his elbow.

After briefly accepting applause, A returns to the chair and turns it back to the first position (where B is sitting over the unsupported back), while B stays at the front of the stage accepting more applause. A then returns to the front of the stage and invites B to play the fast song again.
A says, "Let's play the fast one again", and B agrees. They both take seats.

B must be careful, again, that he does not notice the chair has been turned back to the original position, and that he will again be sitting over the back of the chair.

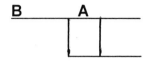

They again play the "Billboard March", at the end of which A jumps up and B falls to the floor. A is super satisfied. He returns to the front of the stage and is explaining to the audience that, "I got him again. Did you see that/ He fall for it again. Ha, Ha, Ha."

He looks behind him to see that B is picking up the chair (over his head) and is coming toward him to crash the chair on him. A runs from one side of the stage to the other, then decides he'd better get away. A exits the stage with B chasing him.

Washday

Number of Clowns:	Two
Characters:	Washer women (Men in drag or actual female clowns) Could also be male clowns doing the wash
Costumes:	Wash dresses, or long johns
Props:	Three buckets, two stools, two dirty rags, popcorn
Stage:	Empty

ACTION: Clown A enters carrying stool and wash bucket (dirty rag is already in bucket). A positions his stool and sits on stage with bucket in front of him. After A is established, Clown B enters carrying two buckets and stool (dirty rag is also in one of his buckets). B sets one bucket aside, positions his stool next to A, and sits down. They exchange greetings.

As each continues to begin his/her wash, B flicks his wet hand in the direction of A, flicking some water on A. B continues innocently doing his wash. A looks around to see if it is 'raining', or where the water came from. When A returns to his washing,…B does water flicking maneuver again. A has same reaction, but then 'realizes' that it was B who was getting him wet.

A tilts his bucket in the direction of B, and splashes some water on B. B looks at self (wet area), looks at A…and then looks at A's bucket…being aware that A intentionally splashed some water on him. This is the beginning of the water splashing escalation.

B takes his wet rag from bucket…forms a ring around the rag with his index finger and thumb…aims rag at A…and slides his 'ring' down the rag toward A. This sends a lot of water in A's direction. A doesn't like it and decides to get revenge, while B goes back to innocently washing his clothes.

A takes his sopping wet rag from the bucket and flings it across B's chest. B, looking surprised, takes his rag out and hits A across chest. A again takes his rag and hits B across chest, even harder. (Each hit on the chest is a bit harder…escalating the 'duel') B now takes his rag out of the bucket…and flings it at A's head.

A ducks and rag goes over his head. A looks up, satisfied that the rag missed him. B then returns the rag from in back of A...and hits A on the back of the head. A is now really mad. He takes the rag...gets it wet...and swings hard at B's chest...knocking B backwards from his stool.

B gets up, returns to his stool, gets his rag wet, removes it from the bucket and spins it over his head in a circular motion...spraying water all over everywhere. He announces, "Spin Dry".

A takes his rag from bucket, strolls over behind B, removes B's hat (if he is wearing one), and wrings his rag over B's head...with water streaming down on B. A then announces, "Ringer"...and returns to his stool.

B is really upset now. He takes his rag out of his bucket, wrings it out, and throws it on the ground. B picks up his bucket of water...and steps behind A. He removes A's hat...and pours the entire bucket of water on A. B...now satisfied that he has won the game...returns to his stool...picks up his rag...and continues to act as if he is washing it in the bucket.

A...seeking more revenge...throws his rag on the ground and calls B's name. B looks in the opposite direction (away from A). A again calls B to look 'over here'. B looks at A, and A throws the entire bucket of water on B...again knocking B off of his stool.

B, really angry, looks around and sees the third bucket on the stage. Meanwhile, A is getting worried. A gets up from his stool and moves a bit away from B. B gets up...grabs the other bucket...and chases A into the audience. After dancing in front of the audience...B throws the contents of the bucket (popcorn) toward A. They chase each other off of the stage.

What Time is It?

Number of Clowns: Two

Characters;   Normal Clowns

Costumes: Normal Wardrobe, but both must be wearing watches.

Props: Watches

Stage: Empty

ACTION: Clown A enters stage for some reason. While he is talking with the audience, Clown B enters and communicates with A. While A is in the middle of something, he asks B to get him a glass of water. B leaves and comes back carrying the glass of water. He is trying to get A's attention, but A is going on with something. Finally A asks B, "What time is it?" B, holding the water in his hand, turns the glass inward toward himself to see his watch, and spills the water all over himself. He is embarrassed and annoyed. A is surprised but continues his business with the audience.

A moment later, A asks B where the water it. B says he'll go and get another glass. He leaves and comes back with another glass of water. As in the first instance, A asks B "What time is it?" B turns the glass toward himself and again spills the water on himself.

A again asks B for water. B is getting smarter and says he'll go and get another one. As soon as he returns he gives the glass to clown A...who holds it in the same hand where he is wearing his watch. This should be the hand nearest to B. B is going to trick A this time and <u>he </u>asks A, "What time is it?" A goes to look at his watch...<u>BUT</u> he turns his hand <u>OUTWARD </u>toward B...(looking at the inside of his wrist)...and spills the water on B...while saying "why it's _____ o'clock". B leaves the scene rather wet and embarrassed.

Whipcracker

Number of Clowns: Two

Characters: Whipcracker (A), Stooge (B)

Costumes: Normal Clown (but whipcracker might wear 'western' wear)

Props: Whip (piece of rope fastened on a length of dowel)

Stage: Empty

<u>ACTION:</u> Clown A (whipcracker) enters carrying his whip and declaring himself to be the world's greatest whipcracker. He can cut anything with just the snap of his whip.
He announces that for today's performance, he will need an assistant. "Are there any volunteers in the audience?"

(He looks around). As he surveys the audience, Clown B enters the stage reading a newspaper. Clown A stops B and asks if he'd like to be his assistant. Clown B indicates 'no' and continues to walk.

Clown A snaps the whip just behind B's behind...and clown B jumps, and agrees to be the assistant.

Clown A is happy and positions B at one side of the stage and directs him to hold the sheet of newspaper directly in front of him with both hands. Clown A explains to the audience that this will certainly be an exciting act, and that he is going to take 10 paces across the stage and be ready to begin. A then proceeds to walk across the stage,... <u>and</u> Clown B walks closely behind him step-for-step...so that when A turns around (at the end of the walk) B is nose-to-nose with him.

Note: It is important that the two clowns rehearse this move, since they must both know just how many steps clown A will take before he turns.

After they are facing each other, Clown A takes Clown B by the back of the coat collar (lifting it, and B walks on his toes), turns him around and marches him back across the stage to his starting position. A then takes his 10 paces across the stage to his 'whipcracking' position.

While A is walking back across the stage, B (still holding the newspaper) leaves his position and goes to the front of the stage to show the audience the pictures in the paper. When A turns around, ready to crack the whip, he notices that B is not there. A goes over to B, again grabs him by the back of the collar (lifting it) and marches him back to his position for the act.

A again crosses the stage to his starting position, does some fancy moves, makes the whip crack toward the paper, and B tears the page in half (slowly) as A yells "Ya Hoo".

A goes to the front of the stage to take a bow. While he is returning to his spot, B goes to the front of the stage to show another picture in the paper to the audience. A turns around,...sees B is gone, and snaps the whip at B. B jumps back, sees A is annoyed, and lifts his own collar from the back and returns to his correct position.

Note: It is very important to have a 1 inch 'starter tear' in the paper before you rip it.

A snaps the whip again, and B tears the remaining part of the paper in half as A yells, "Ya Hoo". (Each time, one remaining half of the paper is used,...thus reducing the paper by half each time)

A takes another bow, and returns to try to slice an even smaller portion of the paper. B holds the paper, A snaps the whip, the paper is torn in half again and A yells, "Ya Hoo". While A is moving to the front of the stage for another bow...B continues tearing the paper in half, this time B is yelling "Ya Hoo" each time he tears the paper in half.

A notices what is happening, goes to B, grabs the remainder of the paper and chases B from the stage.

Prop Construction:

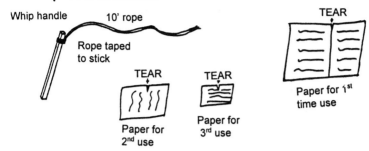

Skits for

Three
Clowns

Space Age Cleaner

Number of Clowns: Three

Characters: Salesman (A), Non-clown (B), Host (C)

Costumes: Salesman (Normal Clown)
Stooge (non-clown Street Clothes)

Props: Double-compartment bucket, Dirty rag, Clean rag, Ketchup, Tabasco Sauce, Mustard, Sponge, Old sport coat, Old Car oil or grease, 'Space Age' potato peeler, 'Space Age' pie mix, small table, misc. Vegematic Type items, box of 'ERASE' (space age cleaner) Cream Pie

Stage: Small Table in center

ACTION: Clown enters stage about to demonstrate the new SPACE AGE CLEANER called 'ERASE'. The clown is portraying a super-salesman, such as you'd see demonstrating the Vegematic slicer at trade shows, fairs, etc. His new 'ERASE' will clean _anything_ from any type of material. He shows a soiled rag to the audience,…pours some of the magic 'ERASE' into _one side_ of the divided bucket. (Clean water is in _both_ sides of the bucket) He then puts the dirty rag into the soapy side and proceeds to 'wash' it. After a few moments, he pulls a sparkling clean rag from the bucket to show the power of 'ERASE'. (Clean rag was in other side of bucket).

After, perhaps a few more demonstrations with socks, etc. someone (a stooge planted in the audience) asks a question about 'ERASE' removing stains from a garment such as a sport coat. The spectator is invited to come up on the stage and is assured that 'ERASE' is truly a miracle cleaner. The stooge is encouraged to allow the clown to 'soil' his sport coat to demonstrate the power of the cleaner. After some coaxing, the stooge allows it. Clown puts items like ketchup, mustard, steak sauce, and most any other item on the coat, making patterns like targets, painting pictures, etc....while 'soiling' the coat. Spectator is somewhat apprehensive about all of this.

After the coat is really a mess, the clown is about to prove the greatness of 'ERASE' and dips a sponge into the soap to show how it works. Wet sponge is applied to the sport coat, making both it and the wearer rather damp. 'ERASE' is unable to remove the stains. Spectator is rather perturbed, but clown insists on trying even more of 'ERASE'. He adds more soap to the water, dips sponge in again, and gets coat even wetter than before, while trying to remove the stains. This only makes things messier. Finally clown asks spectator to 'stand over there' for a moment...while he demonstrates more products.

Spectator takes position on side of stage, and clown proceeds to change agenda and show 'THIS NEW SPACE AGE POTATO PEELER'. Stooge is being ignored and wonders when clown will get back to him. Clown ignores stooge, and tells of greatness of this 'NEW' product.

Stooge gradually moves closer to clown, and asks about his coat. Clown asks him, again, to 'Just stand over there. Can't you see I'm showing these people this new potato peeler?'

Stooge moves back to side of stage, still annoyed. Clown continues to ignore him.

Clown moves on from 'SPACE AGE POTATO PEELER', to 'NEW AND REMARKABLE PIE MIX'. He proceeds to show pie mix box, and takes a large cream pie from under the counter to show the fine product that the mix makes.

Stooge moves closer again, asking about his coat. Clown again asks him to move away, and not interfere. Stooge, annoyed, moves back but continues to sneak closer. When clown isn't looking, stooge takes pie and moves back to side of stage.

Clown is interrupted, on stage, by host for the evening's event. He/She tells clown that she is rather bothered by the fact that an innocent spectator had his clothes ruined by this clown's product....that doesn't even work. Clown makes some haphazard excuse, while stooge is inching closer with cream pie. When stooge is about to hit clown (clown has his back to the stooge), on word-cue, clown ducks and pie actually hits the host person. Both stooge and host are upset as clown realizes he'd better pack up and leave. He packs up quickly and they chase him from the stage.

The Box

Number of Clowns:	Three
Characters:	Game Hustler (A), Stooge (B), Clown in the Box (C)
Costumes:	Normal Wardrobe
Props:	Large box on wheels, Three buckets, Foam Hammer, Play money
Stage:	Empty

ACTION: Skit is based on the old "Shell Game". Clown A enters pushing The Box...with three buckets on top of it. The buckets are inverted, and painted bright colors (red, yellow, and blue). Clown A explains to the audience that he has invented this new money making game, and how all he has to do is find an unsuspecting customer.

At this time, Clown B enters the stage. He is stopped by Clown A and asked it he would like to win some money by trying a guessing game. Clown B agrees. A explains the game to B by showing him there is nothing under the two outside buckets (number 1 and 3), but when he lifts the center bucket (position number 2), there is a clown head there (Clown C) just looking dumb, and smiling...no other movement. Clown A explains that he will put the buckets back on their positions, and then move them around. All clown B has to do to win the money, is to identify which bucket clown C will appear under.

Clown B agrees, and gives some money, perhaps a large dollar bill, to Clown A. A then moves the buckets around (like the shell game), being sure that he does <u>NOT</u> put the same colored bucket over the next hole where Clown C will appear.

Explanation: It is best to have each bucket painted a different color (red, yellow, blue). If Clown C was under the **Yellow** bucket to begin with, be sure he/she is under a <u>different</u> colored bucket for his second appearance…otherwise the game would be too easy. It is also recommended to have a 'pre-set' arrangement for the appearances of Clown C. I would recommend something like…Position 2 for the first time…Position 3 for the second appearance…and Position 1 for the final appearance.

After taking the money, and switching the buckets around…Clown A asks B for his selection choice. B guesses the <u>same</u> color bucket where he first saw clown C. Clown A asks the audience where <u>they</u> think Clown C is. Clown A says something like, "How many think he is under the Blue Bucket?" (Then he shows the blue bucket to be empty). "How many think he is under the Yellow bucket?" (Show empty Yellow bucket). Then show that Clown C is really under the Red bucket.

Clown B is surprised…and wants to try again. Clown A agrees, puts the buckets back into place and collects another dollar from Clown B. A again moves the buckets around, then proceeds to ask the same questions he asked before. Clown B guesses the same color that he last saw C under. Clown A asks the audience for their opinions, shows the empty buckets, then reveals Clown C under the bucket in the #3 position.

Clown B wants to try third time. Clown A agrees, puts the buckets back into place and collects another dollar from Clown B. A again moves the buckets around, then proceeds to ask the same questions he asked before. Clown B guesses the same color that he last saw C under. Clown A asks the audience for their opinions, shows the empty buckets, then reveals Clown C under the bucket in the #1 position.

When A reveals Clown C this time, he is so proud of himself that he goes to the front of the stage (in front of the box) and explains to the audience that he is so good no one could ever outfox him and win the money. While he is doing this, Clown B, who is standing next to the clown head (C), takes a foam hammer from inside the box and beats the clown head down into the box. (C ducks back down as he is being hit). When A turns around he is surprised and baffled as to where the clown (C) went. A looks under the other buckets...can't find C...and finally pushes the box off stage...while B remains on the stage laughing, having outfoxed clown A.

Alternate Ending #2
When the box is pushed off stage, Clown C has come out of the box and is revealed sitting on the stage in back of the box. When C realizes that the audience can now see him, he gets up, embarrassed, and runs off the stage following the box and Clown A.

Alternate Ending #3

After replacing all of the buckets and not finding Clown C...Clown A is bewildered. Suddenly one of the buckets begins to move around. A is surprised and happy. He has now solved his problem and knows where clown C has been hiding. A removes the moving bucket but nothing is there. He bends forward and looks into the hole. At this time Clown C, inside the box, squirts Clown A with a seltzer bottle. A is both embarrassed and mad as he hurriedly pushes the box off the stage.

Special Note:

This skit is also effective as a Parade Skit. One clown pushes the box,...while another clown is inside. Clown behind the box (pusher), lifts the buckets and shows clown head to audience. He tries to get them to guess where the head is going to appear next. After he fools them a few times, he moves the box along the parade route and does the bit again.

Prop Instructions:

Numbers painted on inside of box for planning of routine.
Curtain hangs across back on piece of 1 x 2 which is attached on brackets on each side. Buckets are painted bright colors. Outside of box is also painted bright.

Hangers for curtain

1 2 3

Inside view of box

TOP VIEW

STOPS FOR BUCKETS

Levitation

Number of Clowns: Two or Three

Characters: Hypnotist (A), Dummy (B), and Generic Clown (C)

Costumes: Cape and Turban for hypnotist, Normal Wardrobe for the others

Props: Bench seat, blanket or sheet, sticks with clown shoes on them.

Stage: Bench is set up in center, sheet covers shoes, sticks, and bench.

ACTION: Two or three clowns enter stage, one wearing costume of hypnotist. With a lot of flourish, he indicates that he will hypnotize his assistant. If there is a third clown, they stand in a line with hypnotist facing stooge, and third clown behind stooge.

Hypno throws fingers toward stooge to 'hypnotize' him. Nothing happens and stooge looks like he can't be hypnotized.

Hypno tries again without success. On third try...clown behind stooge falls down as if hypnotized.

Hypno and stooge pick up clown and place him, prone, on the bench. They cover him with sheet or blanket, at the same time placing fake feet (on sticks) out the bottom of the sheet.

Hypno stands back and attempts to levitate him. He rises two or three inches and goes back down. Hypno tries again. Clown rises about 6 inches and goes back down.

Hypno, getting anxious, puts all of the whammy he has into the 'spell' and clown rises to position where he is actually standing while holding fake feet out bottom of sheet. His own legs and feet are covered by the sheet which is draped over his arms and the sticks. He begins to move around (walking) as if levitated.

As he walks by stooge, stooge places foot on bottom of sheet and is pulled off as he walks by, revealing that he is holding the shoes on sticks.

Exposed clown and hypnotist are chased from ring by other clown.

Note: If only two clowns are performing this skit, Hypnotist steps on the blanket or sheet as dummy walks away, thus revealing the shoes on the sticks.

Mary Had a Little Lamb
(the gardner)

Number of Clowns:	Three
Characters:	Museum Guard (A), Stooge (B), Statue (C)
Costumes:	Normal Wardrobe
Props:	Watering Can, Box to stand on, Nursery Rhyme book, Guide's cap
Stage:	Statue is standing on box, holding watering can

ACTION: Clown A (guide) enters with book and says he has this really neat story he wants to tell, but he needs someone to tell it to. Clown B (stooge) enters and says he likes stories. A tells B that this is a <u>new</u> version of <u>Mary Had a Little Lamb</u>. B says that's one of his favorites.

A tells B that he should repeat the lines of the story after he says them, and that he will really like it. (A winks to audience to indicate that something is going to happen to B.)

A begins the story with B repeating each line after A.

A: "Mary had a little lamb"
B: "Mary had a little lamb"
A: "It's fleece was white as snow"
B: "It's fleece was white as snow"
A: "And everywhere that Mary went"
B: "And everywhere that Mary went"
A: "The lamb was sure to go"
B: "The lamb was sure to go"

A tells B that he was good on the first verse, and asks if he would like to learn the second verse. "It's the new part of the story". B says "Yes" and they continue.

A says, "OK. Repeat these lines after me."
A: "Mary went for a walk one day"
B: "Mary went for a walk one day"
A: "Down the shady lane"
B: "Down the shady lane"
A: "When all of a sudden"
B: "When all of a sudden"
A: "All of a sudden"
B: "All of a sudden"
A: "Down came the rain"

While the two clowns have been saying and repeating the second verse, A has been maneuvering B so that B is now standing directly in front of the 'statue'. Statue clown is now holding the sprinkling can over B's head, prepared to pour the water on B as he repeats the last line.

Instead of repeating the last line...B changes the line to:
B: "She had a great pain"

A is surprised because B has changed the line and didn't get the water poured on him. A says, "No...that's not right. Let's try it again." B agrees and they do it again.

A: "Mary went for a walk one day"
B: "Mary went for a walk one day"
A: "Down the shady lane"
B: "Down the shady lane"
A: "When all of a sudden"
B: "When all of a sudden"
A: "All of a sudden"
B: "All of a sudden"
A: "Down came the rain"

This time B says:
B: "She got hit by a train"

A, again disappointed says, "No. That's still not right. We'll try it one more time.

A: "Mary went for a walk one day"
B: "Mary went for a walk one day"
A: "Down the shady lane"
B: "Down the shady lane"
A: "When all of a sudden"
B: "When all of a sudden"
A: "All of a sudden"
B: "All of a sudden"
A: "Down came the rain"

This time B appears hesitant to say the line and seems to have forgotten it and is trying to remember what to say.

A is getting frustrated and in an effort to remind B what to say. (A is now standing in front of the statue, who is holding the watering can.) A says, "Down came the rain...Down came the rain...Down came the rain"

As A says this, Statue pours the water on A, while B is watching. A is all wet and looking at B.

B says, "I've heard that verse before"...and they chase off of the stage.

Long Shirt

Number of Clowns:	Three
Characters:	Normal Clowns (A, B, C)
Costumes:	Two Normal Wardrobe, Clown wearing long shirt (C)
Props:	Long Shirt (tank type top with up to 30' of shirt tail), Over sized pants to hold shirt inside, chair, newspaper
Stage:	Chair in center

ACTION: Clown A enters stage with newspaper...sits down on chair, opens paper and begins to read it. Clown B enters stage, looking in pockets for something. He notices Clown A with newspaper, and assumes it is <u>his</u> paper. He goes to Clown A and gestures that he wants the newspaper. Clown A gestures for Clown B to 'go away'. B steps back a few paces...then again approaches Clown A for the newspaper. Again A tells B to 'get lost'.

B backs up a few steps again, thinks, then signals to audience that he has an idea. B again approaches A but (using large gestures) reaches an arm around A's back and taps A on the opposite shoulder. A looks in the direction of the tapping, slides off the chair in that direction, **BUT** leaves arms, hands, and newspaper in front of the chair. Note: It is important that the newspaper not move, while clowns exchange places on the chair.

B slides onto the chair (vacated by A) and takes the newspaper, allowing A to move away from the chair. A is upset, but moves about 10 feet away from the chair, still looking at the newspaper and being mad that B now has it.

Clown C enters stage (wearing big pants, coat, and long shirt tucked inside the pants), and approaches B for newspaper. The action proceeds just as it did between A and B...with clown C being sent away twice. Finally C 'has an idea' and does to B just what B did to A. C reaches his arm around behind B and taps B on the opposite shoulder. B slides off the chair, leaving paper in front of chair. C slides in where B was on chair.

B and A are now both about 10 feet away from the chair and are visibly upset. They want to fight with C. A is encouraging B to 'take the paper away from C', and, in fact, fight with him. They gesture to each other with fists.

Finally B goes in front of C and snatches paper away from C. C is surprised, and appears to be still looking at the paper, although there is no paper between his hands. C gets up, takes paper back from B and sits back down to read. B again takes paper from C.

C is now mad. Gets up and approaches B. C takes off coat and throws it to the floor. He puts up his fists to fight. Clown B, tries to taunt C by holding newspaper up in the air over C's head. C reaches up for paper but he does not get it. **Note:** *The purpose of this move is to allow C to slip his arms through his suspender straps as part of the reaching up move. This causes the suspender straps to fall from C's shoulders.*

After C reaches up, B throws paper on the floor. This causes C to reach for the FLOOR. This puts C in the 'bending over' position. While C is bent over, B reaches for the shoulder straps of the long shirt, and begins pulling shirt over C's head. A has moved to the <u>back</u> of C to help pull the shirt from the back of C's pants. A is also holding the back of C's pants to prevent C from falling forward. B continues to pull the shirt from C. As he does so, B moves across the stage stretching the shirt and waving it to make it look even larger.

Finally, the shirt is totally removed from C. Clown C stands up to look at the audience and his pants fall down. C notices this...pulls up the pants and chases the other clowns off the stage.

Note: When the shirt is being pulled from C...C should hold both arms outstretched over his head, near his ears. This prevents his WIG from being pulled off with the shirt.

A bit of practice will show why these various recommendations are being made.

Prop Instructions:

Purchase about 7 yards of very bright colored Cotton or knit material…60 inches wide. Any stretchable material will bind up on performer as it is being pulled off. Sew material along seams to make one very long tube. Finally, sew tube to bottom of a very large TANK TOP, or make a tank top from the material. Shirt is placed in extra large pants, 'accordion style' so it will come out properly. When pulling shirt off, it works best if you make it 'wave' as you are pulling it off.

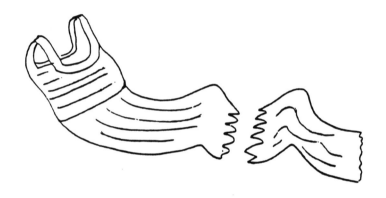

Be sure 'tank top' portion of long shirt is reinforced, and very strong. This area takes a lot of abuse during the start of pulling the shirt off. Sometime the 'straps' of the tank top will tear apart if they aren't reinforced and very strong.

If you use one long piece of material with stripes running lengthwise, it makes the shirt appear much longer due to the visual illusion of length.

Strongman

Number of Clowns: Three

Characters: Strongman (A), Two assistants

Costumes: Special Strongman coat, Normal Clown Wardrobe

Props: Special coat (see drawing)

Stage: Empty

<u>ACTION:</u> Two clowns enter stage exclaiming to audience how they are each the strongest clown in the world...flexing their muscles...posing...etc. A lot of commotion is heard off stage. Both clowns tremble and shake as the real Strongman (can be a smaller clown) enters wearing coat with a coil of rope in each hand.

Strongman is grunting and growling as he stomps to center of stage and declares that he is so strong he can hold both ropes while a number or children (or adults) line up to pull rope (tug-of-war) on each side of him.

Other clowns dare him...and he advises them to get 'assistants' from the audience. About 5 children (or adults) are selected from the audience for each side of the ropes. Strongman tosses ropes out to each side and assistants pick up ropes for the struggle.

On count of 'three' they begin to pull, and Strongman moves from one side to the other as if being pulled. Finally they decide that the must be on the wrong sides, so they switch sides and try again.

Same struggle goes on.

Finally one of the 'assistant' clowns looks off stage, as if getting message from someone. They tell Strongman that he is wanted for a telephone call off stage.

At this point, Strongman walks out of coat and leaves stage, while kids remain holding the rope and showing that rope actually goes right through the coat.

Kids are returned to the audience as the gag ends.

Design of Strongman Coat:
Get about 25 feet of ½" to ¾" rope. Cut two pieces about 2 feet each. These pieces are fastened to the long rope with tape…just where the sleeves of the coat end. This is to give the appearance that you are holding <u>separate</u> pieces of rope in each hand. You also hold a 'coil' of the long rope in each hand. When you have the 'volunteers' on stage, you toss each coil out so they can hang on to the rope for the 'tug-of-war'. They are actually holding the ends of the continuous rope that goes <u>through</u> the coat. You let the extra pieces hang down to appear they are the ends of the rope each side is holding. Be sure your hands are covering the tape area where the ropes are connected.

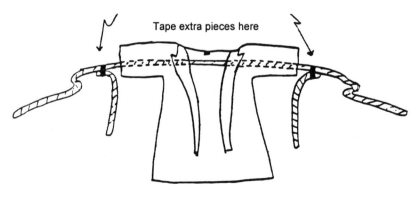
Tape extra pieces here

Fire Fire

Number of Clowns: Three or more

Characters: Tramp, Cleaning Person, and Fireman (or several)

Costumes: Tramp, Fireman

Props: Candle, Hotdog, Frying pan, Matches, Water buckets, Fire hats, Buckets of popcorn, Broom or mop.

Stage: Empty

ACTION: Tramp clown enters carrying knapsack, etc. He wanders around in front of audience, carefully selecting a spot for his 'campfire' (candle). He finally locates a spot, sits down and proceeds to rummage through his stuff. Eventually he gets out a candle, matches, a badly beat up hotdog, and frying pan. He proceeds to make a dinner. He smacks his lips and rubs his stomach in anticipation of a good dinner.

Shortly after he puts the pan over the fire, a cleaning lady appears nearby…sweeping and mopping. She sniffs the air as if trying to determine what she is smelling. She sniffs in several areas, and then notices the clown cooking lunch. She sees the fire of the candle and yells out "Fire, Fire". At this time the firemen enter carrying buckets of water. They throw the water on the clown, dousing his fire on his candle. (Use of a siren at this point is also helpful, if available)

Tramp clown looks bewildered at what has happened. He packs up his stuff, gets up, and looks for another location. Shortly he finds one, on the other side of the area, and goes through the same set up as before. When he begins cooking the hotdog, the cleaning lady reappears, and goes through the same sniffing routine. She then calls out, "Fire, Fire" and the firemen reappear and re-douse the candle and the clown.

The tramp, bewildered again...but determined, seeks another spot for his 'campfire'. He wanders into the audience, looks around and finally sets up his candle right in front of some people. He proceeds to get out the frying pan and hotdog. As he begins 'cooking', the cleaning lady again appears and does the same bit. She yells, "Fire, Fire" and the firemen come running out carrying their buckets. This time they throw the contents of the buckets (popcorn) at the tramp and the audience. Tramp wanders off bewildered and soaked.

Skits for

4 or More Clowns

Mary Had a Little Lamb

Number of Clowns:	Four
Characters:	Museum Guide (A), Stooge (B), Wise Clown (C), Statue
Costumes:	Normal Wardrobe
Props:	Watering Can, Box for statue to stand on, Nursery Rhyme book, Guides cap
Stage:	Statue is standing on box, holding watering can.

<u>ACTION:</u> Clown A (guide) enters stage with book and says he has this really neat story he wants to tell, but needs someone to tell it to. Clown B (stooge) enters and says he likes stories. A tells B that this is a <u>new</u> version of Mary had a little Lamb. B says that's one of his favorites.

A tells B that he should repeat the lines of the story after he says them, and that he will really like it. (A winks to audience to indicate that something is going to happen to B.)

A begins the story with B repeating each line after A.

A: "Mary had a little lamb"
B: "Mary had a little lamb"
A: "It's fleece was white as snow"
B: "It's fleece was white as snow"
A: "And everywhere that Mary went"
B: "And everywhere that Mary went"
A: "The lamb was sure to go"
B: "The lamb was sure to go"

A tells B that he was good on the first verse, and asks if he would like to learn the second verse. "It's the new part of the story". B says "Yes" and they continue.

A says, "OK. Repeat these lines after me."
A: "Mary went for a walk one day"
B: "Mary went for a walk one day"
A: "Down the shady lane"
B: "Down the shady lane"
A: "When all of a sudden"
B: "When all of a sudden"
A: "All of a sudden"
B: "All of a sudden"
A: "Down came the rain"

While the two clowns have been saying the second verse, A has been maneuvering B so that B is now standing directly in front of the 'statue'. Statue clown is now holding the sprinkling can over B's head, prepared to pour the water on B as he repeats the last line.

When B says the line, "Down came the rain"...the statue pours water on him. After getting wet, B steps back and says, "I don't like that game. I'm leaving". A says, "No, don't do that. It's fun. Let's find someone for you to do it to."

B agrees, and they look for another 'dummy'.

At that time Clown C (Wise Clown) enters the sage. B asks C if he would like to play a nursery rhyme game. A, meanwhile, is standing back enjoying the fun...and waiting for B to get C wet.

C says, "OK. I like nursery rhyme games. Let's play."

B says, "The way we do it is that I'll say a line from the nursery rhyme then you repeat it after me. Can you do that?" C says, "Sure" and they begin
B begins the story with C repeating each line

A: "Mary had a little lamb"
B: "Mary had a little lamb"
A: "It's fleece was white as snow"
B: "It's fleece was white as snow"
A: "And everywhere that Mary went"
B: "And everywhere that Mary went"
A: "The lamb was sure to go"
B: "The lamb was sure to go"

B tells C that he was good on the first verse, and asks if he would like to learn the second verse. "it's the new part of the story." C says, "Yes" and they continue.

B says, "OK. Repeat these after me."

B: "Mary went for a walk one day"
C: "Mary went for a walk one day"
B: "Down the shady lane"
C: "Down the shady lane"
B: "When all of a sudden"
C: "When all of a sudden"
B: "All of a sudden"
C: "All of a sudden"
B: "Down came the rain"

While the two clowns have been repeating the second verse, B has been maneuvering C so that C is now standing directly in front of the statue, and the statue clown is holding the sprinkling can over C prepared to pour the water as he repeats the last line.

Instead of saying the line that B just said, C says, "She had a great pain."

B is surprised because C changed the line and didn't get the water poured on him. B says, "No, that's not right. Let's try it again." C agrees.

B says:
- B: "Mary went for a walk one day"
- C: "Mary went for a walk one day"
- B: "Down the shady lane"
- C: "Down the shady lane"
- B: "When all of a sudden"
- C: "When all of a sudden"
- B: "All of a sudden"
- C: "All of a sudden"
- B: "Down came the rain"

(Statue is again prepared to pour water on C when he says the line, but again C again changes the line) This time C says: "She got hit by a train"

B, again disappointed says, "No. That's still not right. We'll try it one more time." C agrees.

- A: "Mary went for a walk one day"
- B: "Mary went for a walk one day"
- A: "Down the shady lane"
- B: "Down the shady lane"
- A: "When all of a sudden"
- B: "When all of a sudden"
- A: "All of a sudden"
- B: "All of a sudden"
- A: "Down came the rain"

This time C appears hesitant to say the line and seems to have forgotten it and is trying to remember what to say.

B is getting frustrated and in an effort to remind C what to say. B (now standing in front of the statue, who is holding the watering can.) says, "Down came the rain…Down came the rain…Down came the rain"

As B says this, Statue pours the water on B, while C is watching. B is all wet and looking at C.

C says, "I've heard that verse before"…and they chase off of the stage.

Cheerleader

Number of Clowns:	Four or more
Characters:	Smart Clown (cheerleader), Tramp, Two firemen
Costumes:	Cheerleader, Firemen, Tramp
Props:	Cards with letters on them (C-L-O-W-N-F-I-R-E), 2 buckets of water
Stage:	Empty

ACTION: Cheerleader enters and attempts to get audience involved in cheering. He/She holds up each letter with the normal cheer of:
  "Give me a C" (Audience responds with "C")
  "Give me an L" (Audience responds with "L")
  "Give me an O" (Audience responds with "O")
  "Give me a W" (Audience responds with "W")
  "Give me an N" (Audience responds with "N")

  "What does it spell?" (Audience "CLOWN")

  "Louder" (Audience "CLOWN")

While cheerleader is doing this, tramp clown has been watching. It is important that tramp has been visible to audience so they are aware that he is on the scene. After cheer, tramp decides to try his hand at it. He brings his own cards out...and tries to get audience to do his cheer.

  "Give me an F" (Audience responds with "F")
  "Give me an I" (Audience responds with "I")
  "Give me an R" (Audience responds with "R")
  "Give me an E" (Audience responds with "E")

  "What does it spell?" (Audience "FIRE")

  "Louder" (Audience "FIRE")

  "Louder" (Audience "FIRE")

At this point to firemen clowns run out and throw water on the cheerleading tramp clown...and they chase each other off.

Construction Company

Number of Clowns:	Six
Characters:	Mother, Bratty Child, Const. Foreman, Three workers
Costumes:	Construction outfits and hardhats, small kid, mother
Props:	Two sawhorses, breakaway ladder, board (for swing), plank, chair, tarp, wheelbarrow, hardhats, blueprints, foam blocks, step-ladder, single ladder
Stage:	Chair for mother, Blocks for kid

ACTION: Mother is sitting in chair 'knitting' while child is playing on the floor with foam blocks. Foreman enters with blueprints. Mother and foreman look at them. Brat comes over and steals prints away. Other workers are spreading tarp on floor. Mother goes over to child to scold him and get prints back. After workers spread trap, one goes past chair and moves it about 10 feet. Mother sits down, on 'missing' chair and lands on floor. She gets up, looks around for chair and sits. Brat pulls tarp, causing clown standing on it to fall.

Worker brings in step ladder and sets it in the center of the stage or ring. Brat throws block at worker and hits him on the back. He falls. Mother gets up and scolds brat. Worker moves chair. She again sits and falls on the floor. She gets up, finds chair, and sits down. Other workers enter with 2 sawhorses, and place a plank across the top with one end hanging over.

Worker is standing near the end of the plank. Brat comes over and pushes him. He pushes back. Brat pushes him back and he sits on end of the plank, causing it to flip up and hit foreman who is just coming over.

Both foreman and worker are on the ground. Another worker enters carrying board under his arm. He turns around (board swing) and just about hits the other two workers, but they duck in time. They sit up...board swings back, and knocks them down again. They get up and take the board out.

Worker begins to climb step ladder. He climbs it and sits on top. Brat comes over and starts to push ladder...first pushing it...then pulling it back...then finally pushing it over. Clown on top rides ladder to floor and does forward roll. Worker enters with 'breakaway' ladder and goes for brat's neck. Rungs of ladder fall out and onto floor without hurting kid.

Note: Breakaway ladder is made with only top three rungs glued in. Other rungs are held in with velcro on their ends and they 'break away' when they are touched.

Two workers come in with another single ladder carrying it between them above their heads. They encourage kid to hang on to the rungs, and they lift the ladder high. Worker places wheelbarrow under kid. Workers tickle kid and he falls into the wheelbarrow, which could be filled with foam or soap. They wheel him off with the others chasing.

Teeterboard

Number of Clowns:	Up to six or seven
Characters:	Circus tumblers (Flier, Jumper, Catcher, 3-4 tumblers)
Costumes:	Tank tops, shorts, tights, tennis shoes
Props:	Teeterboard, ladder (4 foot), tumbling mat, lawn chair, 4 - 3' pieces of PVC
Stage:	Empty

ACTION: Entire troupe enters running in single file line…with last two clowns carrying rolled up tumbling mat. When they reach center stage, all stop except last two…causing mat to push into last clown and each clown hits the one in front of them. The result is a knocked down pile of clowns.

They get up…place mat on floor…and all run to front of mat facing audience…extend arms outward, and yell 'HEY'…as real teeterboard acts perform.

Then they proceed to perform "over and under". This is a tumbling act on the mat. The clowns form two lines behind the mat. 1st clown on right line falls to center of mat and rolls toward left side. 1st clown on left line jumps over rolling clown, falls to mat, and rolls toward right side. Next clown on right line jumps over rolling clown, falls to mat, and rolls to left side. Next clown on left lines jumps over rolling clown, falls to mat, and rolls to right side.

All clowns in lines continue this sequence until everyone has done maneuver twice. At that point they get 'confused' and everyone ends up in a pile on the mat. They scramble around...get up...go to front of mat, extend their arms outward, and yell "HEY".

They return behind mat and form a Pyramid. Three clowns get on their hands and knees side-by-side on the mat. Two clowns get on the backs of the three clowns. They are also on hands and knees. One clown mounts the top of the pyramid and stands with arms extended. When this clown yells "HEY", he/she jumps down to the back of the pyramid...the two bottom-outside clowns roll outward, and the pyramid collapses. They all get up...go to the front and yell "HEY".

After the bows, two clowns get the teeterboard and set it behind the mat. Another clown gets the ladder and places it at one end of the teeterboard. Largest member of the group climbs to top of ladder, while smallest member gets on bottom of teeterboard. They seem prepared to 'launch' small member into the air. Catcher clown stands behind board to 'catch' the flier. Other clowns stand near catcher as spotters.

The clown on the ladder and the 'flier' argue about their positions. Ladder clown indicates he/she wants to be the 'flier'. They finally agree and large clown takes place on bottom of teeterboard, while small clowns climbs to top of ladder.

Once in this position, large clown looks around, sees catcher is ready, and slaps hands on thighs indicating he/she is ready to 'fly'. Clown on top of ladder indicates to audience that flier will do a two-and-a-half backward somersault to the catcher. Flier concurs.

Ladder clown looks at audience and laughs very loud about the 'possibility' of this happening. Clown on ladder finally actually jumps on top of teeterboard,...and (hopefully) it doesn't move...due to the weight of the large clown on the bottom. They both look surprised.

Small clown walks down teeterboard to large clown, pushes him/her off of board. They argue. Large clown slaps small clown...and catcher clown (who was not hit) falls down.

They return to the board and get ready to try again. This time 'catcher' has placed lawn chair on long connected sections of PVC so that chair is about 12 feet in the air.

Flier looks around, sees height of chair and indicates "NO"...it is too high. Catcher removes lowest section of PVC, lowering chair to about 9 feet.

Flier looks around again. It is still too high. Catcher removes another section lowering it to 6 feet. Ready to go, flier looks around again...still not satisfied with the height. Catcher removes another section lowering chair to about 3 feet. Again indicating they are ready, flier looks back...and once more says the chair is too high. Catcher removes the remaining position of the PVC, and sets chair on the ground, while he goes to collect the PVC pieces.

While he is doing that, large clown leaves teeterboard, goes to chair and casually sits down. Others are surprised...run to chair and form semicircle around large sitting clown. They all look to audience and yell, "HEY". This is followed by all clowns getting up and running off stage.

Seascape...a story

Number of Clowns:	Many (up to 11 or 12)
Characters:	Narrator, sun, clouds, fisherman, bathing beauty, waves, lighthouse, fish, boater, sea gull, breeze, tide
Costumes:	Fisherman, White Cap, Bathing Beauty.
Props:	Large empty Tide Box, Clouds, Fishing Pole, Sun
Stage:	Empty

ACTION: Narrator enters stage and informs audience that he/she is going to paint a beautiful picture for them. He begins by gesturing to them that his picture will be a beautiful landscape. He points out the imaginary lake, the wonderful sand beach, and points out the clear blue sky. He then says that only a few nice fluffy clouds move across the sky.

Clown enters stage holding large 'Cloud' in front of face. An other clown (sun) enters stage <u>behind</u> (and hidden by) Cloud-clown. These two clowns take positions at up-stage center.

Narr: "The sun begins to peek out from behind the clouds."

'Sun' cloud looks out, and holds sun from behind the clouds.

Narr: "Now that we have the sun and a few clouds…we need a lighthouse to protect the ships from the rocks that might be near the shore. And here's our lighthouse".

'Lighthouse' enters and takes position downstage center (front). Lighthouse rotates, opening mouth each time he faces the audience. This indicates the 'light'.

Narr: "A slight breeze begins to blow across the waters".

Clown enters side of stage blowing to create 'breeze'.

Narr: "The blowing breeze causes the water to have slight waves."

Clown enters and goes forward and back several times making 'wave-like' motions with his hands. On the third time across…clown puts on white cape (whitecaps) and does one more pass.

Narr: "And a seagull circles the lighthouse…and returns out to sea."

Clown acting as a bird…enters from side of stage, circles lighthouse, and leaves stage.

Narr: "And every beach must have it's Bathing Beauty"

Bathing Beauty clown enters, sets up picnic, and lies on beach.

Narr: "The waters beckon to the boaters. Even the ones with oars."

Clown enters sitting and moving as if in a boat...across the stage, but being careful not to 'boat' into the 'beach' area.

Narr: "The fisherman comes down to the waters' edge to try to catch the very elusive fish

Fisherman enters with pole...pretends to cast line into the water. Fish enters from other side of stage...pretends to be 'hooked' and finally gets loose and swims away.

Narr: "But as evening sets in...the waters recede and the Tide comes in". (nothing happens).
Narr: "I said...in the evening the Tide comes in". (nothing happens).

Narr: (louder) "I said in the evening the TIDE comes in."

Clown enters from side of stage carrying huge box of TIDE.

Narr: "No, not that kind of tide. Get out of here".

All clowns run from stage with narrator chasing them.

Restaurant

Number of Clowns:	Up to 12
Characters:	2 Chefs, 2 Waiter(esses), Maiterdee, 5 Customers, Cop, Bus boy, Photographer.
Costumes:	Normal Clown Wardrobe, Waiter aprons, Chef hats, Cop Uniform
Props:	Tarp, Crab, Foam Pizza, Seltzer bottle Card Tables, 5 folding chairs, plates and cups, tablecloths, long-shirt, soap pies, menus, signs (optional), foam salad items, salad bowls, large foam sandwich
Stage:	Two card tables set up, with three chairs at one, and two chairs at the other one. Chairs are placed so that all clowns are facing the audience. Signs are erected on sides of area, tarps are under everything.

ACTION: As gag opens, the two clown 'chefs' are in front of the tables tossing (juggling) a mixed salad of foam props. After about 15 seconds, the two waiters enter and put tablecloths on the tables. (Chefs exit when waiters appear). After tablecloths are on, waiters get plates and cups and put them on he tables.

Maiterdee escorts couple number one to table with two chairs, seats them and gives them menus. Waiter comes by to talk with them briefly and leaves. Maiterdee seats couple number two at table with three chairs, and gives them menus.

Waiter comes by and asks if they would like water. They say yes, and he proceeds to fill glasses (cups) with water form seltzer bottle. Some water gets into the glasses, but most gets on the customers. Waiter leaves.

Maiterdee seats third customer at table with couple number two. Man customer gets up (to express courtesy) at third customer is seated. While he is standing, waiter moves his chair to the other table. He sits, and falls to the floor. Maiterdee chastises waiter, and returns chair behind customer. While apologizing to customer, waiter again moves chair to vacant spot of the other table. Customer again falls to the floor. Maiterdee gets chair, puts it back, and kicks waiter out.

Waiter #1 returns to table with food (large sandwich, etc.) for customers. Waiter #2 returns with crab for one customer, and large foam pizza for man customer. They struggle with pizza (see pizza skit), and finally let it fly. Man customer is upset and wants to fight. He takes off his coat and confronts waiter. They proceed to get into fight and waiter pulls long shirt from customer. When pants fall down, customer pulls them up and returns to chair at table.

Both waiters return to tables with dessert (soap pies). Waiter #2 places one in front of each female customer, and hits male customer with one pie. Male customer sees other female laughing at him, and pushes her face down into pie on table. More pies appear, and begin flying with everyone getting hit.

Finally Cop (one of the chefs who has returned wearing cop uniform) appears, blowing whistle and clears everyone out. They chase out of the area.

Twelve Days of Clowning

Number of Clowns: Seven to twelve

Characters: New clown, Piano player, Powder clown, Prop clowns

Costumes: New Clown wears "New Clown" T-Shirt, Others wear Normal Wardrobe

Props: Piano with door on back, Large and Giant powder puffs, 3 - 6 boxes and cans of simulated make-up, 10 Large shoes, 15 clown noses, 20 striped socks, 20 wigs, 24 pairs of gloves, 28 hats, 16 linking rings, 36 juggling balls, 20 walk-around props, 22 balloons on sticks, 12 cups of water on tray.

Stage: Piano sits on one side (near center) with chair for piano player. ('Powder Clown' is inside of piano)

ACTION: This skit is based on the song "The Twelve Days of Christmas." You can write your own words or use the words listed here. After the words are written, it is important to have them recorded on a cassette tape, for use during the skit presentation. No one actually sings during the skit. The "NEW CLOWN" merely <u>mimes</u> the words as the tape is playing. **

Skit begins as Piano Player enters stage, followed by NEW CLOWN. Piano player takes seat at piano preparing for intro. to song, and NEW CLOWN takes place at front of stage to 'sing' this ballad. As each 'day' of clowning is mentioned, a prop-clown brings the item to the NEW CLOWN from back stage. It is important that the item <u>reach</u> the NEW CLOWN just as it is mentioned in the song. Not all items are brought out every time.

Determine in advance what running pattern the prop-clowns will use to enter and exit the stage, since there will be confusion, and having a predetermined running pattern will avert possible collisions.

Select a small sized clown to work 'inside' the piano. This clown (Powder Clown) comes out of the piano every time the song says "...and some make-up and a big powder puff." When he/she comes out, they are carrying a large powder puff, filled with powder, and they hit the NEW CLOWN immediately after the word 'puff'.

It is advisable to have a can of powder and a small flashlight inside of the piano to assist the small clown in seeing what he/she is doing.

On the "12th Day", the small clown brings out the Giant powder puff and hits the NEW CLOWN with that. After being hit with the giant puff, the NEW CLOWN drops his pants, and runs off the stage chasing the powder clown. Music concludes, and piano player gets up and takes bow, as if nothing had happened and piano player was actually the star.

Suggested Words for the Song:

On the **First Day** of clowning, the boss clown gave to me…some make-up and a big powder puff.

On the **Second Day** of clowning, the boss clown gave to me…Two Giant Shoes, and some make-up and a big powder puff.

On the **Third Day** of clowning, the boss clown gave to me…Three fake noses…Two giant shoes…etc.

On the **Forth Day** of clowning, the boss clown gave to me…Four Striped Socks, Three fake noses…etc.

On the **Fifth Day** of clowning, the boss clown gave to me…Five Different Wigs, Four striped socks, etc.

On the **Sixth Day** of clowning, the boss clown gave to me…Six Pairs of Gloves, Five different wigs, etc.

On the **Seventh Day** of clowning, the boss clown gave to me…Seven Funny Hats, Six pairs of gloves, etc.

On the **Eighth Day** of clowning, the boss clown gave to me…Eight Linking Rings, Seven funny hats, etc.

On the **Ninth Day** of clowning, the boss clown gave to me...Nine Juggling Balls, Eight linking rings, etc.

On the **Tenth Day** of clowning, the boss clown gave to me...Ten Walk-Arounds, Nine juggling balls, etc.

On the **Eleventh Day** of clowning, the boss clown gave to me...Eleven Circus Balloons, Ten walk-arounds, etc.

On the **Twelfth Day** of clowning, the boss clown gave to me...Twelve Cups of Water, Eleven circus balloons, etc.

Construction Directions for Building Piano:

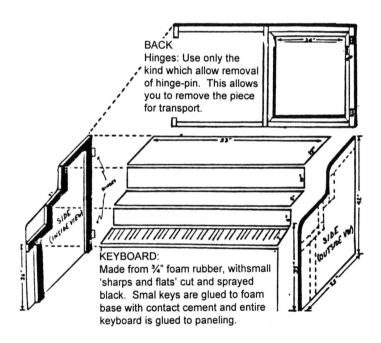

Please note that in the following schedule, <u>all</u> items are not brought out <u>every</u> time. There is enough confusion and plenty of props, so the audience is not even aware of the fact that all props are not always being brought out. Because of the number of prop-clowns, this is the only feasible way to do it. On the last day (twelfth day) ALL PROPS **ARE** BROUGHT OUT.

** Pre-recorded Cassette Tape for this skit is available from the author.

The pattern for delivering the props to the NEW CLOWN on the stage is as follows. This is set up for four (4) prop-clowns. B - C - D and E. (A is the powder clown)

Item	Day (referred to in song)											
	1	2	3	4	5	6	7	8	9	10	11	12
Puff	A	A	A	A	A	A	A	A	A	A	A	A
Make-Up	B											C
Shoes		D		B			C				B	B
Noses			C		D		E		B			D
Socks				E		E		E		E		E
Wigs					C		C				C	C
Gloves						B		B		B		B
Hats							D		C		D	B
Rings								D				E
Balls									D	D	D	D
W/A's										C		C
Balloons											B	B
Water												D

121

Additional Skit Instruction

The author of this book is available for group seminars and training about skit performance techniques and skit writing. He is also available for numerous additional topics relating to the field of clowning and performing.

In addition to winning many awards for skit writing and performing, he has appeared in many circuses, and performed stage shows in the United States and Europe.

For a list of available classes and to schedule seminars or lecture demonstrations, contact:
> Barry DeChant
> 14209 Ingram
> Livonia, MI 48154
> (313) 522-7878